GOOD COP/BAD COP:

Mass Media and the Cycle of Police R

by

Jarret S. Lovell

Willow Tree Press, Inc.
Monsey, New York, U.S.A.
2003

For Michael G. Maxfield
The consummate mentor

For Phyllis Schultze
The unsung hero of criminology

ISBN: 1-881798-49-6.

Cover design by Dave Musso of Spaciousmind Art & Graphic Design.

CONTENTS

continued...

FOREWORD

Good Cop/Bad Cop... is about the media, the police, and their patterned intimate relationships. Jarret Lovell explores these changing patterns here in several intriguing ways, examining both the media and the police. They are engaged in a configuring dance, each learning from the other. It appears at this point that the media are more shapers than shaped.

How do we know about the police in a democracy — what they do where and when and how? Knowledge of policing is of two kinds — the knowledge coming from the imagery of the mass media and knowledge based on personal experience. In the absence of close contact and interactions with police, mediated experience seems to trump personal experience, especially when the media are dramatic, engaging, and produced and disseminated for profit.

Let us begin by describing the police mandate, or what they are expected to do, and what they expect of themselves. The police, as Albert J. Reiss, Jr. (1974) argues, aim to penetrate whilst avoiding being penetrated. Metaphorically, this means that police seek to guard their secrets, the fundamental basis of any group, and to gather, systematize, and use the secrets of others. In the past, the police were highly dependent on paid informants, *agents provocateurs*, random patrol, and watchful citizens. These arrangements worked well to buffer the police and establish a symbolic presence in societies that were still in large part based on face to face interactions, undifferentiated and non-technological. They work less well in mass societies based on mediated communication where the media can rapidly peer into and behind the boundaries of people's lives and organizations.

Now consider the media as part of the burgeoning, oligopolistic unreality industry (Mitroff and Bennis, 1993; Gitlin, 1980). The media mirrors itself and its own concerns, and is not a mirror on the "world" in any relevant sense. Even a cursory look at the media, their news, features, docudramas, sports and reality shows, reveals that programs are not designed to educate, inform, or produce a critical populace, but to insure profits and to entertain. The new omnipresent imagery of the media sustains a deep, abiding and cynical ambiguity (Purdy, 2000). Viewers bring to the imagery a context, assumptions, history, sensibilities, even political interests and imagery that do not and cannot stand alone, even when stripped and decontextualized by editorial and technical efforts. As Marshall McLuhan (1964) first argued, television is a hot medium — the medium is the message. What McLuhan means is that television induces people to see themselves through watching it, and that it is powerful and seductive because it allows self-investment in what is seen. We see ourselves being the Terminator, not Arnold Schwartzenegger. Television thrives on the display of richly evocative ambiguity. Its ambiguity is its power and attraction. Meaning depends on framing activities at "both ends" of the transmission-reception process — what is sent and what is received. Surely, we are in an era of exploding imagery of glorious variety.

What has changed in police-media interaction in the last 50 years or so? The mobility, speed, world-wide satellite networks, and rapacity of the media combined with widespread use of simple and cheap hand-held cameras and recorders have altered the environment of imagery in which we live. The perverse, deeply cynical ability of the media to grasp images anywhere in the world, loop or reuse them in a new context, edit, change the context in which they are shown, and sustain a peculiar entertaining if vulgar "reality," remains unchallenged. The police are vulnerable to new forms of penetration and in turn possess new forms of penetrating and monitoring the movements and words of individual citizens and groups. Policing practices are being captured now, recorded, archived, and disseminated — often instantly. Citizens, in addition, see others in new ways, see others watching and they watch the watchers. The back stage aspects of the police drama are made more visible, not only because they have adopted new technology such as video and audio devices in cars, but because of the media's reduced response time and citizens' uses of new electronically-based technologies.

The degree and quality of media attention has changed as well as the medium. Lovell describes the extent to which the police have always been media-sensitive, and how they are now caught in a world wide web of electronic communications, and swim in a sea of images. Images of police, cops, good and bad, he shows, are and have long been a function of the media's attention to policing. The police provide a lasting and durable (cultural) surplus value that can be used variously to entertain, titillate and threaten. An important contribution of this book is that it reinforces this point from an historical perspective, as well as describing the new-found media manipulation capacities of the police.

Unfortunately, in a mediated society, images can spin away from the ground, and images compete with other images — not experience — as a source of validation for our hunches, worries, fears and diverse anxieties (Sparks, 1992). It is thus difficult to identify how such performances are decoded by audiences — are they instrumental, expressive, or strategic communication? When the sources differ, noise abounds, and the framing of the messages is unclear, the intention is unclear.

This formulation, in spite of media cooperation and police information officers, means that no one knows with certainty how messages will be understood. What are the differences in impact and credibility of the source in proactive police communications (advance information, warnings about repeat victimization risks, aid to citizens seeking police assistance), reactive police communications, responses to calls, and media events, and those that "spin out of control" and require "damage control"?

Increased media hegemony means that the media, from the police perspective, represent both a threat and a promise. The threats are many. Consider recent examples of horrendous axial media events noted by Lovell, the shooting of Amadou Diallo, and the raping and beating of Abner Louima in a New York City police station. There are also public revelations as a result of media and/or citizens' filming of police actions, a powerful example being the citizens' video that became the source of a world-wide television frenzy showing the beating of Rodney King, Jr. The media can bring vast benefits to police, such as serving as a public bulletin board, reprinting their press releases as fact, covering news conferences and providing tips to the police. The media uncritically touted the announced effectiveness of police efforts in reducing official crime statistics and elevating celebrity chiefs in the 1990s. Some of the media's attention is ambiguous. For example, the media seized on and publicized the fashionable phrase "community policing," a rhetorical move designed to persuade and convince whilst making minimal structural changes in the basic practices — random patrol, investigation and responding to 911 calls.

In many respects, the police are ambivalent about the media. They want to appear to be helpful, ready to inform the public and often ask for their assistance and information on crime, yet they see the public as naïve, and view the protection of their procedures and secrets as essential. The media are not fully trusted to present the police perspective on events, and media management techniques are new ideas in policing, still being worked out, and many of the officers have had to create the role of police information officer as they go along. Lovell's quotes from police information officers are rich and telling and hopeful. As the quotes show, police media people relish the ways in which they can convince the media to elevate and dramatize their successes — the "perp" walk, where innocent people are paraded and shamed before the media as they enter the courthouse or leave the jail; the televised news conference after a successful drug raid and seizure; the arrest of a notorious public enemy. They also know that cases that become public concern, such as rapes or a series of shootings, if not solved quickly, change the game of media-police interaction. From a waltz, it is transformed into a form of slam dancing. In such public cases, the police try to spin the spinners, frame things for the framers, and keep their cherished secrets cloistered. In all such important cases, the police are tempted to lie to the media, conceal facts, distort them, mislead the media with "tips," pit the media against one another if possible, and keep their own cards very close to their vests.

One perspective on the dramas that Lovell reveals in this engaging book is to see them as a comment on authenticity and secrecy in mass societies. When the police stage a media event, hold a press conference, release "news," or statements, they are acting to stage authenticity (MacCannell, 1973). That is, they seek to preserve their deeper secrets and information by staging a little theatre, much like those performed by the colonial dames at Williamsburg, a city that exists as the Rockefeller Foundation imagined it to be. Such performances feed the media and the public while they sustain the police pretense of possessing secret, deep and incisive knowledge.

An important question which Jarret Lovell wrestles with throughout the book is: to what degree do developments in media relations produce or result in changes in policing? The police-media connection, like the challenge to public agencies by business and the profit rhetoric, creates ironies. The aim of policing is to increase trust, and the media may well increase public trust and the legitimacy of the police, but if the media are distrusted, does this reduce the legitimacy and trustworthiness of the police? This book, the first to look inside the police-media relationship, gives us a window into the new questions we face in mediated societies.

Peter Kirby Manning
Brooks Professor of Policing and Justice
Northeastern University
Boston, MA

REFERENCES

Gitlin, T. (1980). *The Whole World Is Watching*. Berkeley, CA: University of California Press.

MacCannell, D. (1973). "Staged Authenticity." *American Journal of Sociology* 79(November):589-603.

McLuhan, M. (1964). *Understanding Media*. New York: McGraw-Hill.

Mitroff, I. and W. Bennis (1993). *The Unreality Industry*. New York: Oxford University Press.

Purdy, J. (2000). *For Common Things*. New York: Vintage.

Reiss, A.J., Jr. (1974). "Discretionary Justice." In: D. Glaser (ed.), *The Handbook of Criminology*. Chicago, IL: Rand McNally.

Sparks, R. (1992). *Television and the Drama of Crime*. Milton Keynes, UK: Open University Press.

ACKNOWLEDGMENTS

The study that produced several chapters of this book was supported by a grant from the U.S. National Institute of Justice (2000-IJ-CX-0046). I would like to thank Robert Kaminski for his administrative oversight during the funding process.

Countless members of the law enforcement and media communities were essential to understanding the nature of police-media relations. I would like to acknowledge the nearly 200 police departments that participated in the survey, as well as the four departments that granted me complete and free access to their media relations offices and staff. I would also like to acknowledge the reporters, camera crews and news editors who agreed to speak with me regarding the rewards and challenges of working the police beat.

The idea to study the influence of media on policing and — conversely — the influence of policing on the media stemmed from many conversations and exchanges with Professor Michael Maxfield. I would like to thank him for helping me to cultivate the ideas that ultimately became this project. I would also like to thank Professors George Kelling, Mercer Sullivan, Steven Chermak, and Peter Manning for their comments and criticism during the development of the theoretical framework that constitutes this book.

Through her oversight of the Criminal Justice/NCCD Collection at Rutgers University, Phyllis Schultze provided much assistance in locating and obtaining important documents and readings necessary throughout the writing process. She also happens to be a terrific person and a great companion when rummaging through used bookstores.

A number of colleagues proved most helpful in assisting with this project. Justin Ready provided immeasurable input into the study upon which this book is based, and his contributions to the present text are evident throughout this book. In addition, Sharon Chamard, William Sousa, and Jennifer Sumner provided editorial and substantive comments to various drafts.

I would like to acknowledge the entire faculty and staff within the Division of Political Science & Criminal Justice at the California State

University, Fullerton for the assistance they have provided throughout the writing process. In particular, I would like to acknowledge Frederica Register, Denise Hall and Bunny Casas for helping me to get a jump-start on the writing process. I would also like to acknowledge Alan Saltzstein for his encouragement and mentorship throughout.

I am grateful to have in Rich Allinson an editor whose interest in, and knowledge of the subject matter assisted greatly in the development of the project. His comments and critiques have improved my work drastically. Any and all shortcomings are solely a reflection of my editorial decisions.

Finally, I would like to acknowledge the guidance and support provided by my family and friends. It is because of their encouragement that this book became a possibility.

INTRODUCTION

"It appears that some officers took the law into their own hands when they thought no one was watching..."
Kweisi Mfume, NAACP President[1]

"The video is why we're here."
Johnnie Cochran, Attorney at Law[2]

In early 1991, media imagery proved to be the catalyst that placed the issues of racism, abuse of force, and police reform onto the national agenda. George Holliday was standing on the balcony of a nearby building when he videotaped the beating of Los Angeles motorist Rodney King at the hands of four police officers taking place on the street below. The events featured on his 81-second videotape capped off a high-speed chase between the Los Angeles Police Department (LAPD) and King, who refused to stop when signaled by officers. When the chase came to a final conclusion, officers delivered to King 56 strikes of the baton and six kicks to the head, producing injuries that included skull fractures, as well as brain and kidney damage. One day later, Holliday delivered his videotape to a local news station, and by the next news cycle, images of the beating were broadcast to an international audience (Wood and Fiore, 1991).

Without the video footage as evidence, it is unlikely that the beating of Rodney King would have ushered in any talk of police reform. In fact, unaware that their actions were caught on videotape, the officers filed an incomplete incident report that made no mention of King's serious physical injuries. Moreover, then-Los Angeles Mayor Tom Bradley had not publicly challenged any LAPD account of use of force in years (Lawrence, 2000). But the video was presented as evidence of abuse, and with it came widespread appeals for sweeping changes to the LAPD specifically and to law enforcement more broadly. With the events on the video not easy to dispute, Mayor Bradley now called for a government investigation into the event (Wood and Fiore, 1991). As a result,

(1) the city convened its Christopher Commission to investigate allegations of abuse by the police; (2) citizens' organizations began a campaign to remove Daryl Gates from his position as LAPD chief; (3) nationally, the Congressional Black Caucus called for a federal investigation into racially-based abuse of force both in Los Angeles and elsewhere; and (4) heeding the call, the U.S. Justice Department announced that it would expand its investigation of abuse by the LAPD to include federal complaints of abuse. All of this occurred not in spite of the videotape, but because of it.

A little over a year after the images of the King beating surfaced, its grainy images still fresh in the public mind, the acquittal of four of the officers by an all-white jury sparked race riots in the heart of the city and ultimately brought about a change in the racial composition of the department leadership. Willie Williams — an African-American police veteran and outsider to the LAPD — was subsequently appointed the city's new police chief, vowing that the department would "open its doors" to the citizens of Los Angeles through minority recruitment of officers and expanded community policing (Serrano and Rainey, 1992). Indeed, the yearlong debate surrounding the videotaped beating helped popularize the concept of "community policing" as a way to improve the quality of police-citizen interaction, and it helped to bring about the 1994 congressional mandate calling for the Justice Department to maintain a database of incidents of police misconduct (Lawrence, 2000).

Some 11 years later, the July 6, 2002 beating of 16-year-old Donovan Jackson was dubbed "Rodney King revisited" and "another Rodney King" by such news outlets as MSNBC and Black Entertainment Television (BET). All of this was the result of a videotaped altercation between Jackson — an African-American male who is reportedly developmentally challenged — and Inglewood police officer Jeremy Morse, who is white. The incident began when two Los Angeles Sheriff's Department deputies approached Coby Chavis at an Inglewood gas station to investigate expired tags on his car. A struggle began when Jackson, Chavis's son, came out of the station mini-market and ignored orders by deputies to halt. The events that followed were videotaped from a hotel window across the street, and feature the use of force by Morse and a second Inglewood officer against Jackson, both of whom had arrived on the scene to provide the deputies with assistance. Its duration only a few seconds, when the videotape begins Jackson is seen lying down on the pavement with his hands cuffed behind him. Officer Morse next lifts a limp Jackson off the ground and allegedly slams him onto the hood of the police car. What happens next on the video is equally disturbing, as Morse is seen punching Jackson in the face before the footage comes to a conclusion (Associated Press, 2002).

Like the Rodney King videotape, media coverage of the Donovan Jackson beating generated numerous demands for police organizational reform. Within hours of the event, the videotape received national attention. Almost immediately, the National Association for the Advancement of Colored People (NAACP) issued an appeal for the U.S. Justice Department to take immediate action to investigate possible civil rights violations on the part of Inglewood police. Grass roots organizations mobilized en masse and staged protests and hunger strikes in front of the Inglewood Police Department. The son of civil rights activist Martin Luther King, Jr. appeared outside police headquarters to lend his voice to those of angry protestors who were calling this a case of racial profiling. The Attorney General of the United States requested that the Civil Rights Unit of the Federal Bureau of Investigation (FBI) conduct an inquiry into the beating. Activist Reverend Al Sharpton called for the firing and prosecution of Officer Morse. Inglewood Mayor Roosevelt Dorn called for the installation of video cameras in police cars as a means of keeping check on officers and verifying their police reports.

All of this mobilization for national reform occurred not because of the countless allegations of abuse of force throughout the United States, but because of one videotape brought to public light. In fact, as in the Rodney King case, but for the presence of that video the beating of Donovan Jackson would likely have gone undetected, especially since Bijan Darvish — the second Inglewood officer at the scene — was indicted by a Los Angeles County Grand Jury for filing a false police report that made no mention of the beating. At a news conference discussing the incident, attorney Johnnie Cochran, who is representing Jackson in the case, thanked the man who filmed the incident for bringing it to the nation's attention. Asked to comment on the alleged filing of a false incident report by Officer Darvish, Cochran noted, "He didn't know there was a video. That's why he lied in the report. The video is why we're here."

*   *   *

The purpose of this book is to cast the mass media as central to police administrative and strategic reform. Its central premise is that new forms of media technology generate new forms of information about police practices, giving police officials little choice but to alter their law enforcement practices. Stated simply, innovations in media technology (i.e., print, the television, the video camera) increase the amount of information about the police that is available to the public. This book argues that each "era" in the evolution of police practices was precipitated by advances in media technology that provided the public with new information about the police. More often than not, this information has undermined the political and social legitimacy of police, resulting in movements toward image, organizational, and even strategic reform.

Of course, technological advances often arise as a result of social necessity, and media therefore must necessarily be only one part of the myriad social and political forces that exert pressure upon civic leaders for accountability. For example, and looking back in history, the technology of moveable type did not bring about the Protestant Reformation any more than gasoline created the automobile. Certainly, attempts at achieving both religious reform and motorized mobility predate their finalization as successful endeavors in the printing press and cylinder engine. Nevertheless, the printing press allowed Martin Luther's writings to be widely circulated and to accumulate a critical mass, thus advancing ecclesiastical reform movements, just as gasoline quite literally proved the catalyst necessary for the motor vehicle. Technology alone does not cause social movements, but it certainly provides the fuel necessary for their realization.

It follows, then, that the technologies comprising the mass media are not the sole cause of police reform. Rather, a complex web of social, political, and economic arrangements among officers, administrators, political leaders, and the public shape contemporary police practices, and these factors similarly account for much of the impetus that ushers in a new phase in policing. Yet media cannot be characterized as anything but significant, as it is through media that information regarding these political, social, and economic arrangements is communicated both among the leaders and to the public. It was television, after all, that broadcast images of the police acting out against protestors during the 1960s, thus placing civil rights and an end to the Vietnam War on the national agenda. And it was the hand-held video camera that made "community policing" a national catchphrase after a bystander recorded the beating of Los Angeles motorist Rodney King. In short, it must be acknowledged up front that media do not "cause" police reform, as the social conditions necessary for reform always predate the catalyst; but media are effective in directing enough attention to the potential causes both before and more significantly after the pivotal event, thus allowing for police reform to occur.

UNDERSTANDING MEDIA

An awareness of how media contribute to police reform requires a broad understanding of what media are and how they function in the political arena. *Media* are those *technologies* that stand between a source and recipient of information, allowing for communication between the two to become possible. Media are any technologies that facilitate the acquisition and exchange of information. In the strictest sense, then, the pencil, the telescope, and even the light bulb are forms of media technology because they eliminate the barriers that typically constrain the gathering and dissemination of information in much the same way that the telegraph and the telephone do today. But while these inventions are important for helping us to conceptualize media as technologies, their potency pales in comparison to the "mass" media. The *mass media* are those communication technologies having the capacity to disseminate information to *multiple recipients* simultaneously, perhaps even to millions of people. The printing press, television, film, and the Internet all represent technologies of the mass media.

Collectively, these technologies comprise *the media*, an *industry* whose economy is predicated upon the acquisition and distribution of information to the public. For example, the news media are an industry that stands in the middle between government officials and the voting public and that ideally disseminate information between the two, though more often than not the flow of information is only one way. Newspapers and news broadcasts, magazines, and now the Internet all represent forms of the news media. Likewise, the entertainment media typically distribute fictional information created by storytellers and artists to a mass audience. Movies, television, and children's comic books are examples of entertainment media. Taken as a whole, the mass media industry comprises those responsible for the collection and dissemination of news, information, and artistic talent to a wide audience. Since there is an infinite supply of information available to mass media but only limited resources for distribution, the media industry possesses enormous influence over political and social discourse in society.

Today, we live in a mediated society where telephones, e-mail, and the television facilitate communication. Because it is through mass media that the public most often interacts with its community officials, the media industry can serve as a powerful source for political accountability through the shaping of public opinion. In fact, one of the most significant political changes to occur throughout the twentieth century has been the increase in attention paid to public opinion as a result of the mass media. Individuals seeking a successful political career must, more than ever before, possess a detailed understanding of communication media and must package their behavior in accordance with the demands of the mass media to maintain a satisfactory level of public support. Therefore, in an era dominated by live television debates, impromptu press conferences, even participation in Internet town hall chat rooms, technology is rewriting the rules that govern politics and leaving an indelible imprint upon the manner with which civic leaders govern.

This rewriting of political norms means that those who wish to govern must never become complacent in their position of power. Instead, civic leaders must periodically reconstruct a public persona that adheres to the demands of new and evolving media technology. The constant restructuring of the political image is part of a broader reflexive feedback loop that has become central to virtually all areas of political and social life, including police work. Each day, powerful individuals receive information about their job performance from public opinion polls, voter turnout results, and from media pundits whose newsreels and social commentary help to determine the popularity of political figures. In turn, civic leaders reform their public practices as a response to the evaluations they receive. When media coverage suggests that the public is failing to buy into the image pitched their way, those in power must out of necessity take steps to restage their public performances.

The rise of mass media and the media industry, then, has produced a political culture dominated by the advertising, marketing, and promotion of one's self-image. As early as 1922, Walter Lippmann wrote about a revolution that was taking place in the creation of political consent through the means of modern communication (Lippmann, 1922 [1997]).

Edward Bernays (1923) wrote extensively about the centrality of image and the public persona in political life. Specifically, he called attention to the importance of mass media in crystallizing public opinion, since it is the newspaper, the photograph, and radio that deliver the actions of political leaders to the public. By the end of the 1950s, the staging of political events had become the business of America's civic leaders, according to historian Daniel Boorstin (1992). He noted that the most successful politicians had been those most adept at using the media to create what he called "pseudo-events" or political events staged for the purpose of self-promotion.

But while much has been written about the mass media's influence on governing and political behavior, relatively little has been written about the influence of the mass media upon the everyday behavior of the police and upon the influence of mass media on the organization and reform of police practices.[3] Instead, scholarly treatments tend to focus upon the role of the police in shaping the content of news media (e.g., Ericson et al., 1989; Chibnall, 1981; Hall et al., 1978) or conversely, on the role of the news media in creating various constructions of policing (e.g., Lawrence, 2000; Kappeler et al., 1998). There are, however, several reasons why one might expect the mass media to play a substantial role in shaping contemporary police practices and bringing about police reform. Let us take a moment and quickly outline the arguments for a focus upon the mass media as an influential factor bringing about change in the nature and scope of police practices.

The police are the most visible of government representatives, and with this high visibility come increased opportunities for public accountability. As the police are frequently featured in the headlines of daily newspapers and in the plotlines of Hollywood films, the media have a unique opportunity to play an essential role in bringing about a change to the strategy and structure of policing. Indeed, by assessing the quality of police practices through news coverage and by calling for organizational change when clearly necessary, media help pave the way for police reform. Thus, the period following the highly publicized beating of Los Angeles motorist Rodney King proved essential in bringing about a necessary focus upon the need for community policing initiatives nationwide (Lawrence, 2000). Of course, calls for community-oriented policing certainly predated news coverage of this highly politicized media event. It was, however, the technology of the hand-held video camera that allowed for this case of police abuse to be brought to national attention, and undoubtedly, it was concern on the part of police that countless additional citizens were in possession of this video monitoring technology that solidified the community-policing paradigm.

One reason the police are so prominently featured in the media is because they are given enormous public powers that are rather contradictory in the context of a free society. As Herman Goldstein (1977) notes, the ability of the police to arrest, search, and detain citizens under the threat of force is necessarily disruptive to freedom. Moreover, this authority is delegated to individuals at the lowest level of government bureaucracy and in conditions with little direct regulatory oversight (Wilson, 1973). For this reason, citizens are understandably suspicious of the police and of many police practices. At the same time, the public is dependent upon the police to provide them with many protections and services. Citizens even tend to support funding initiatives for an expanded police force despite their many suspicions. At the center of this contradiction is the mass media, whose primary responsibility ideally involves the rectifying of the free society/police presence paradox through the monitoring of police power as part of the "fourth estate" mandate of a free and public press. In short, as a result of the unique powers vested in members of law enforcement, their activities are frequently monitored and portrayed in the media, leaving them susceptible to calls for reform. The police recognize this and have, when necessary, reformed their practices to meet the demands placed upon them as a result of widespread media coverage.

An examination of the relevance of media to police practices is also warranted by the sheer fact that the history of the police so closely parallels that of the mass media. The first "modern" police forces in the United States began to appear in the early to mid-1800s during a time of rapid urbanization, immigration, and industrialization, contributing to social instability and anomie (Uchida, 2001). The steam-generated "penny" press made its debut in America at about the same time (Davidson et al., 1976), and the stories featured in these new penny papers naturally gravitated toward the very issues relevant to the urban centers. Certainly, the presence of new and (loosely) organized police forces was a central concern to city dwellers, who tended to possess a mistrust of official authority. When the muckraking journals provided a platform for progressives, the police were by no means exempt from calls for widespread reform. In time, visual imagery would come to dominate new media technology. It is not surprising, then, that the police have been and continue to be so prominent in cinema and on television, for the badge, the uniform, and the patrol car are designed as visual reminders of the authority of the state. Even today, when "reality" entertainment is popular among the public for being far more dramatic and compelling than Hollywood fiction, one can easily forget that programs such as *COPS* and *Real Stories of the Highway Patrol* ushered in the reality-television genre.

In sum, the modern police force has been the target of media scrutiny since police first established ranks in urban centers. Their high visibility, coupled with their incredible political authority, renders them perfect candidates for public accountability. Moreover, the image-laden essence that is bound up in police work makes them attractive subjects for entertainment and news drama. Since the police are not immune to scandal or controversy, the development of new media technologies has uncovered previously concealed or unpublicized scandalous police practices, resulting in newspaper headlines and Hollywood caricatures that have questioned the very legitimacy of police practices and have addressed the need for change. While it is certainly true that any examination of the evolution of policing cannot occur without consideration of the broader political, social, and economic factors of the time, it is the goal herein to argue that media technology and the media industry are among those political factors essential to an understanding of police organization.

Of course, the assertion that media are a force for reform is no small argument, and it is one that is difficult to make given the manner with which the media routinely function in a capitalist society. To be sure, the technologies that comprise the mass media are inherently progressive when placed in the proper hands, since they can democratize the citizenry by providing them with means to disseminate their opinions and perspectives about powerful leaders and hold them publicly accountable. Yet the deregulation and privatization of media ownership under a capitalist economy necessarily produces an antidemocratic climate where access to the vehicles that can influence public opinion is limited to a powerful and specific few. Today, some six global corporations control the international flow of news and information (Bagdikian, 2000). Moreover, as the drive for profit requires that the media become the domain of advertisers and paid sponsors, it becomes increasingly important for news outlets and even motion picture studios to adopt a stance of thematic objectivity to attract the widest possible audience (McChesney, 2000). What results is an increasing dependence upon "official" versions of events and an abandoning of more partisan and challenging interpretations that might offend potential audiences.

The media industry, then, typically exerts a form of political hegemony in that their messages tend to support the established political and social order. Far from a progressive force, the media's dependence upon information from the political leadership and its support for the status quo renders it a tool that is subject to use or manipulation by those who control them or by those with direct access to media outlets. And it is in this sense that the historical dependence upon the police by the news media can be a very bad thing, for unlike those who are policed and have little access to media, members of law enforcement are routinely called upon by news reporters to serve as official news sources and to assist in the production of entertainment media. Therefore, and as a result of frequent and direct access to media outlets, law enforcement personnel can and do use media for the purpose of ideological hegemony.

But if mass media are routinely under the control of the political and social establishment, then how can they possibly contribute to political or social reform?

THE "CULTURAL LAG"

Historically, power has rested among those with the ability to master the art of communication while controlling the flow of information. In the pre-literate, oral societies of early Greece, citizens having political power were those proficient in the verbal communication of poetry. Poetry was not merely expressive but a political necessity whose devices of meter and parallelism allowed leaders to more easily recall the history of Greek politics (Havelock, 1963). In scribal societies, the skills of literacy were limited to a selected few and scribes were thus treated as royalty. The medieval Catholic Church was able to maintain its authority due to the limited number of people who could read the scripture and offer alternative interpretations of the gospel. Today, the media are hot commodities sought after by powerful figures who seek to control the flow of information and shape public opinion through media ownership.

The interrelationship of media and authority suggests that any loss of control by those in power over the flow of information will threaten their authority and legitimacy within the social order (Meyrowitz, 1986). Yet a loss of information control is precisely what occurs when a new form of media is introduced into society. New forms of media are necessarily dangerous to authority because they alter the amount and content of information available to the public. As a new medium, the printing press brought about increases in literacy rates while affording an opportunity for new and revolutionary ideas about Christianity to be widely disseminated, ultimately bringing about the Protestant Reformation. The new medium of radio altered social arrangements by allowing for communication over long distances and to a wide audience, but it also transmitted dangerous and propagandistic messages in times of war. Television has altered the traditional family hierarchy by making children more susceptible to messages parents would otherwise conceal, thereby inhibiting the ability of parents to parent (Postman, 1994). At the same time, it changed the rules of political campaigning by elevating the importance of appearance in political discourse, as Richard Nixon clearly learned following the first ever televised presidential debate. Today, the Internet has become an arena for the mass circulation of information to the public that is often unregulated and unverified by government officials.

New forms of media, then, are inherently threatening to the status quo because they alter the patterns of social and political communication. Their introduction into society necessarily creates a "cultural lag" (Fischer, 1992) during which time those holding authority are only beginning to learn of the new medium's potential for subversive use, and they have yet to conform their practices to meet the demands of this new technology. Therefore, it is during this cultural lag when new media are best suited to bring about political or social reform through the dissemination of new forms of knowledge to disenfranchised members of society. In time, those with political or economic power come to recognize the danger inherent in new media, and they actively take steps to harness the potential of these media by co-opting their capabilities and using them for their own gain, but not before some damage is done.

For example, by the 1920s, large economic interests had bought most of the penny presses and muckraking papers that helped to democratize the urban landscape by making access to information affordable, but not before the newspapers placed numerous progressive reforms — including police reform — on the national agenda. The nation's top policing officials ultimately proved effective in establishing a mechanism for the regulation of motion pictures, but not before the industry challenged sexual conservatism, questioned prohibition, and criticized law enforcement. And today, the police, still clearly threatened by the pairing of the video camera with the news media, are quickly acquiring cameras of their own to be placed in patrol cars and used as exculpatory evidence in high-profile cases. Even the Internet, which was once hailed as, "the most transformative technological event since the capture of fire" (Croteau and Hoynes, 2000, citing *Harpers Magazine*, 1995) for its ability to empower grassroots political groups and interactive town hall meetings, is increasingly becoming a commercial domain run by the same financial giants that control newspaper and television ownership.

MASS MEDIA AND POLICE REFORM

At key times in the history of policing, law enforcement has fallen victim to this technological cultural lag. As will be seen in subsequent chapters, advances in printing technology, the rise of the motion picture industry, and live and remote television broadcasts have upon their introduction posed significant challenges to the overall legitimacy of the modern police, and in many respects they still do. Even an advanced understanding of, and rich familiarity with, the demands of the media do not wholly diminish their potential to cause harm to the police organization. Thus, for example, the news media typically favor official institutions because these government agencies offer journalists expedient access to legitimate news sources. But reporters often feel uneasy about their dependence upon government agencies for they do not want to serve as uncritical publicists for government practices (Gans, 1979; Bennett, 1990; Lawrence, 2000). Therefore, they may just as easily abandon their dependence upon police officials during times of political scandal and turn to challenging voices to provide the news story. True, it was video and then television that first brought the Inglewood beating incident to the public eye, but even print, which is hardly a visual medium, amplified the story with boldface headlines declaring "Beating" and "Officers Face Felony Counts" that appeared alongside a repro-duced still of the video footage.[4]

Still, it is new media technology that clearly poses the greatest threat to the political legitimacy to public leaders, for it is new media that gen-erate new information and distribute its content to previously untapped audiences. When this occurs, it simply becomes impossible for officials to conduct business as usual without reforming their conduct to meet the demands of their new and sometimes critical public. When advances in printing technology disseminated information about police involve-ment in political machines, when motion pictures took artistic license with the very real problem of organized crime, when television brought racism and domestic unrest directly into the living room, and when video and now the Internet promise to make every citizen a keeper of the police, the police have had little choice but to recognize the need for reform. Media may not have been the catalyst in every instance, but they no doubt have hastened the process of change and served as a reminder to law enforcement of the dire alternative of stagnation.

It is important to note that the assertion that media are a factor con-tributing to police reform rests upon one rather large assumption: that the police bureaucracy is amenable to significant changes in the manner in which they conduct business. Like other large organizations, urban police departments often share many of the same features that have come to epitomize all bureaucratic agencies, such as the specificity of tasks by personnel, the delegation of responsibility to separate yet inter-connected divisions, and the flow of information through a complex chain of command (Walker and Katz, 2002). These factors alone pose challenges to the communication and implementation of widespread administrative and policy changes. Add to this the observation that, be-cause of their size or their complexity, bureaucracies can become iso-lated from the culture they purportedly serve, resulting in their imper-meability to external pressures. This kind of isolation from the commu-nity has been especially problematic within various law enforcement agencies, where a police culture marked by values and beliefs distinct from the broader community's is said to arise.

All of this combines to create what appear as rather insurmountable obstacles to achieving significant police reform. In fact, many police scholars view the prospects for reform as rather limited. Thus, Gold-stein (1977:328) argues that in many respects, "the likelihood of achieving significant change seems remote." This, he suggests, is the result of the traditional approach to reform that places the onus for change exclusively upon the top police administrator. More significantly, he suggests that, "the conditions of immediate concern to police" continue to be those related to crime fighting. Sparrow et al. (1990) echo this sentiment by identifying the "police-as-crime fighter" myth as among the many obstacles that make reform difficult, especially when the public has come to expect the police to perform as crime fighters. More recently, Zhao (1996) has argued that the police view organizational change as both traumatic and unsettling, perhaps explaining why the core focus of police organizations has changed little over the past half century and why the shift to more service-oriented models of policing is met with resistance.

Nevertheless, all of these authors are in agreement that police organizations have, and do, change. Despite the "agonizingly slow" rate of progress inherent in law enforcement agencies, Goldstein remains positive. Observing that, "More progress was realized in policing in the [1960s], when the police were operating under great pressures, than in any other period," in the end, he comes to the conclusion that the prospects for police reform "may be brighter than initially appears to be the case." Sparrow et al. (1990) are more direct, calling the appearance of organizational immutability "an illusion." Because of the importance and clarity of their defense of the existence of police reform, their assessment will be quoted at length:

> American policing went through a major crisis in the first half of [the twentieth] century that changed its character enormously.
>
> The responsibilities, purposes, methods, and social support of policing have all changed. Policing as we know it today is the result of those changes, not a historical accident but certainly a historical artifact.
>
> Without knowledge of this history, observers of the police could be forgiven for assuming that the current nature of policing was preordained. Even so, there would be another reason for skepticism. Policing is young; the police as we know it have existed for only about 150 years…There is no reason to think that its ends are correct and immutable, or its means effective and mature (pp.30-31).

OVERVIEW OF THE BOOK

This book provides an account of those occasions when new media served as a force for police accountability and reform. It argues that at key times in the history of policing agencies have fallen victim to technological cultural lag, allowing for the media to serve as vehicles for the protest of police practices, resulting in the adoption of new administrative or organizational practices.

The study begins with an examination of the nature of police work. Specifically, it situates policing as part of the constructionist framework, where the meanings and responsibilities of law enforcement are derived through a process of symbolic interaction. Because people more often interact with the police indirectly through the mass media, this book illustrates how the media have become an essential component to the legitimacy of contemporary police practices and police reform.

In addition to focusing upon the theoretical and behavioral aspects of policing, this book examines the theoretical aspects of media, as well as the influence of media upon police behavior. While most commentators suggest a strong and powerful link between media and social behavior (e.g., media violence and social aggression), this book will suggest more subtle ways that media influence policing patterns through the reinforcement of policing definitions and roles, including the construction of the police as crime fighters, the "good cop" fictional persona, and the very real "bad cop" of police work.

The book concludes with a description of a new paradigm of policing. This paradigm recognizes mass media as a conduit to the public. Following the tumultuous events of the 1960s that were broadcast live, many police departments began to hire public information officers (PIOs). The job of the PIO is to serve as the primary media spokesperson for the department, to monitor the police image, and to actively promote the image of the police through regular media appearances, the construction of press releases, and regularly held news conferences.

The conclusion also provides a discussion of the cultural contradictions of police work, particularly in an era of mass media. One such contradiction is the extreme level of popularity that surrounds "fictitious" rogue cops. These "Dirty Harry" characters that fire their weapons indiscriminately have proven extremely popular among audiences, and they have converted the bad cop into a new form of "good cop" persona. Judging from contemporary media, it appears as though the public at some level *expect* police to shoot first. But if media really do influence socially aggressive behavior, then what influence does the Dirty Harry image have on actual police practices?

A NOTE ON DATA AND ANALYSIS

This book includes data obtained by the author as part of a larger study funded by the U.S. National Institute of Justice. The purpose of the study was to elicit information about the frequency and quality of police-media interaction, about the policies that dictate the means by which police officials and their officers communicate directly to the public through the news media, and finally, about the influences and impact of mass media on police administrative and street behavior.

The research methodology included a 10-page questionnaire distributed to 255 municipal police departments nationwide that yielded a response rate of 76% (194). Information garnered from the survey was used to identify four police departments that served as ethnographic case studies. Data were obtained from interviews with police chiefs as well as with department media spokespersons and local news reporters, and first-hand observation of police-media interaction obtained during "on-the-scene" live remote broadcasts, press conferences, and patrol ride-alongs. Approximately 100 hours of observation were conducted across all research sites.

The analytical framework used throughout this book is informed by conclusions drawn from the aforementioned study as well as from theoretical and research writings examining the impact of new media and technology on behavioral and cultural change. It is the intention of this book to apply an interdisciplinary perspective that combines communication studies, sociology and film studies to the study of law enforcement so that researchers can fully comprehend the myriad cultural influences that shape the nature of contemporary police practices.

NOTES

1. "NAACP Denounces The Inglewood Police Department for Use of Excessive Force." *NAACP News* (press release), July 9, 2002. (Available at: http://www.naacp.org/news/releases/inglewood07902.shtml.)

2. "Inglewood Cops Post Bail, Remain On Leave," by Frank Buckley on CNN. Posted July 19, 2002. (Available at: http://www.cnn.com/2002/LAW/07/18/inglewood.indictment/index.html.)

3. Two notable exceptions are Surette (1995) and Perlmutter (2000). In his study of new police recruits, Surette presents data suggesting that news media coverage of a high-profile shooting involving a Hispanic police officer exerted a significant influence on the expectations of Hispanic new police recruits, but not on new recruits from other racial backgrounds. Perlmutter's four-year observation of police behavior uncovered subtle ways that media coverage of police practices both defines and reinforces certain aspects of police behavior. Both studies are discussed in Chapter 2.

4. "2 Policemen Indicted in Boy's Beating: 2 Officers Face Felony Counts," by Beth Shuster and Anna Gorman. *Los Angeles Times*, Orange County edition, July 18, 2002, A1, A27.

1. POLICING IN AN ERA OF MASS MEDIA

At a time when guns, drugs and gangs occupy city streets, the following memorandum was delivered to patrol officers during morning roll call instruction at one of the nation's largest police departments:

> We live in a media world! Everything and everyone is fair game for the roving video camera; there's a profit in it! Whether it's a professional news station shooting some dramatic footage in order to win the ratings race or a home movie enthusiast selling his/her tape to the highest bidder, video pays! All one needs is a television to see how popular unstaged "video happenings" have become, and the evening news is only one of many venues for them. Today, shows like *World's Wildest Police Chases* proliferate the airways.
>
> As police officers, we must realize that the nature of our work makes us a natural and very attractive subject for reality-based television programs (news and otherwise). Therefore, it is more important than ever to maintain a professional demeanor. We simply do not have the luxury of letting our guard down. We owe it to ourselves, our fellow officers, our department and our families, not to become a negative story. There are cameras everywhere! Let them catch us doing the job the way we were trained.[1]

The urgency of these cautionary words was in reference to a controversial video featuring a high-speed car chase that ended in what reporters were calling a case of excessive force. The police, however, were not so sure. Documented earlier that week by a helicopter news camera, much of the video's content was undisputed: the pursuit, the abandoning of the car by the suspect, his subsequent apprehension. Yet some key details remained unclear, details that could make all of the difference to the public when assessing police integrity. For example, as the video was filmed from a sky-view and at a less than optimal distance, it was uncertain whether the officer repeatedly struck the suspect with his fist, as alleged. Similarly, it was difficult to ascertain whether the suspect attempted to grab hold of the officer's gun — an act that may or may not have precipitated the officer's behavior — as was also alleged.

This department, however, would never have to comment on the case to reporters. The officer on the videotape was not one of their own, and the footage was of another agency. Still, the police at morning roll call understood the implications of what they had seen on the video. They knew that to maintain their legitimacy, they needed to be prepared to respond to all negative imagery produced by media technology, whether the imagery be real or fictitious, whether of their own activity or that of another department. They knew that the nature of police work makes them, as they put it, "a natural and very attractive subject" for news and entertainment media and a constant target of calls for reform. And perhaps above all, they knew that, like the work of politicians, stage actors, and others who perform in public, police work is not only about that which is, but also about that which is perceived.

EMERGING ISSUES IN POLICE WORK

In our highly advanced technological society, the legitimacy of the police is dependent upon mass media. Each day, the police appear in news headlines and video clips, in big budget Hollywood movies and network television dramas. And now, police even appear as stars in weekly "reality" cop shows. Graber (1980) has shown that crime stories receive nearly three times the frequency of news coverage as the presidency, Congress, or the economy in some news outlets (e.g., the *Chicago Tribune*), and an equal percentage of coverage in others (e.g., ABC National News). Of course, the police feature prominently in these crime stories, as news angles tend to focus upon police investigations, official calls for public assistance, and the successful apprehension of criminal suspects. Chermak (1995) notes that crime news stories tend to focus upon the early stages of the criminal justice system, with police activities comprising the bulk of story content. Entertainment media likewise center upon the activities of police and other crime fighters. Today, television shows about crime and law enforcement comprise roughly 20% of all prime-time programming across the three major networks (Surette, 1998), while cop shows and movies airing in syndication on such cable networks as Court TV and TNT likely increase the prominence of law enforcement within media. Stated simply, police practices are a staple of the mass media.

Despite the prominence of the police within the mass media, most citizens do not have direct or daily contact with police officers. Instead, they encounter law enforcement indirectly through media. Mass media, therefore, play a dominant role in the formation of citizen evaluations of local police, and public support for police practices is often dependent upon media coverage of law enforcement. Not only did the Rodney King videotape mobilize political leaders and grassroots organizations for change, it also had a negative impact on public opinion surrounding the police in general. One study (Lasley, 1994) found levels of public support for the police across all races evidencing a sharp decline in the months following the tape's emergence. Tuch and Weitzer (1997) examined Los Angeles area public opinion polls in the months prior to and following several highly publicized cases of police excessive force, including a 1979 shooting death of a black woman, the 1991 Rodney King beating, and a 1997 videotaped beating of two Mexican immigrants. As expected, at every time period in the study, whites were more supportive of the Los Angeles police than were blacks. However, also as expected, approval ratings for all respondents declined after each publicized police event, with the largest declines recorded among African-American residents. Jefferis et al. (1997) examined the influence of a widely publicized 1995 violent arrest of a teenaged African-American male on citizen perceptions of police abuse of force. Using data from the Greater Cincinnati Survey covering the period 1984-1995, the authors found that a single, highly publicized and controversial event negatively impacted public perceptions of police use of force, with the impact greater for minorities.

In his detailed description of the social organization of policing, Manning (1997) describes the symbolic construction of police work as equal in importance to what the police actually do. He suggests that the construction of "appearances" represents a fundamental component of routine policing since officers are the most tangible embodiment of the State. Police, in a sense, represent theatrical actors who work feverishly to create an impression that appearances are real. As a result, they seize upon particular aspects of their activities to dramatize their effectiveness as the keepers of social control, and through the management of appearances they struggle to create a sense of law and order within the body politic.

While Manning's (1997) description of the symbolic nature of policing is among the most direct, other police scholars have alluded to the symbolism inherent in routine police work. The police officer has been described as a "Rorschach in uniform" whose "occupational accouterments — shield, nightstick, gun and summons book — clothe him in a mantle of symbolism that stimulates fantasy and projection" (Niederhoffer, 1969:1). Van Maanen (1974:104) refers to the lack of affect displayed by many officers as a symbolic "mask to fend off the perceived curse of doing society's dirty work." He describes policing in terms that suggest the ultimate goal of law enforcement is to create an impression of law and order irrespective of actual circumstances. And Loader (1997) argues that police primarily wield symbolic, rather than coercive, power. Like Manning, he argues that police use symbols and rituals for instrumental purposes that assist in the overall police mandate to maintain the appearance of order.

Policing, then, may be seen largely as a symbolic action. Like many other functions of government, it is designed to establish confidence in the overall health of the collective, even if and when society is at its weakest. As a president or prime minister must maintain dignity in his/her public appearances at all times, and especially during times of national crisis, so too must the police uphold the appearance of law and order, for the police represent the health of the State at its most tangible and proximal level. The appearance of control therefore represents a fundamental component of successful policing, for as Manning suggests, police work symbolizes much more than the mere enforcement of laws.

This book expands upon Manning's constructionist framework of policing by illustrating how the proliferation of media technology continues to add new dimensions to the management of police appearances. But while Manning (1997:36) suggests that police officers "may not understand their actions" in terms of the social construction of the appearance of order, it is argued herein that police today clearly understand the constructionist aspects of what they do, for they are acutely aware of how popular their performances have become on the evening news. In fact, many departments now employ full-time public information specialists to work with media for the purpose of enhancing their public image. Thus, police are not only passively involved in the construction of appearances through the daily rituals of ceremony and spectacle, as Manning suggests, but as will be illustrated in subsequent chapters, they are now actively involved in the creation of the police image.

At the same time that police officials work to construct an image of policing in the media, the nature and patterns of much police work are in fact a reaction to media constructions of policing. To understand this requires an understanding of how media impact social and political hierarchies. Mass media function as extensions of the senses that allow individuals to see and hear things about their community representatives previously concealed from public audiences (McLuhan, 1964). As such, the television camera becomes an omniscient, voyeuristic eye; the audio recorder becomes a highly perceptive eavesdropping ear. With this type of political checks and balances available to the public sector (Meyrowitz, 1986), it has become a necessity for social leaders to restructure their behavior to meet the demands of a media-driven society. With members of law enforcement regularly featured in mass media, police have had to constantly repackage themselves to address the criticisms in newspaper headlines and Hollywood characterizations to keep in step with new information and image-producing technologies.

All of this suggests a cycle of performance reflexivity at work. Reflexivity represents a process wherein people shape and reshape their behavior according to evaluations of their presentations. Each day, individuals and organizations script future behavior to satisfy the demands of a critical public. As an example, individuals often engage in reflexivity through simple, everyday practices such as checking one's hair in a mirror or asking a friend to comment on the aesthetics of personal attire. For public figures, reflexive evaluations periodically occur through public opinion polls and voter results during elections. But day-to-day evaluations of public figures stem from media coverage of their routine actions. Government officials are likely to "play up" favorable media appearances by repeating well received sound bites or reemphasizing popular themes. When media images reflect appearances that are unpopular among the public and therefore threatening to public leaders, the leaders are likely to restructure appearances to alter the reflected imagery.

The ability of media to portray law enforcement contributes to performance reflexivity (Manning, 2001), providing law enforcement officials with commentary on the level of public support surrounding various police practices. Police respond to media imagery by either reforming their strategies or, more commonly, by taking steps to simply alter their appearance. In turn, as it is a job of the media to both reflect and characterize the patterns and habits of government officials, media then represent and reflect these changes back to the police, who then decide either to abandon or adopt these revisions to their public appearance. The thesis of cultural reflexivity as it pertains to both police and the media, therefore, asserts that policing is both a reaction to, and an influence on, media imagery. In short, police performance (what police actually do) and police performances (the constructions of police work) are mutually reinforcing.

THE CONSTRUCTIONIST PARADIGM

The assertion that the police actively create a public persona situates policing as part of a constructionist paradigm and builds upon an impressive body of theoretical writings about the dynamics of social and political life. The constructionist paradigm of reality is rooted in the theory of "the sociology of knowledge," or more simply, in the idea that a relationship exists between human thought and the social context in which it arises (Berger and Luckmann, 1967). In the daily construction of meaning social interaction is central, as it is through shared experiences that definitions are formed and adopted. In the same way that language requires a shared acceptance of the use and connotation of a given word, the parameters of appropriate human behavior emerge through informal, collective decision making. It is this informal nature of the social construction of reality that sociologists refer to as "symbolic interaction" (DeFleur and Ball-Rokeach, 1989). Symbolic interaction, therefore, occurs when individuals form definitions about the nature of themselves and their surroundings through the largely non-verbal communications (i.e., gestures, reinforcements) that they receive from others.

Groups, too, play an essential role in symbolic interaction and in the broader construction of reality. In our complex and diverse social structure, the group provides an identity and ideology as we attempt to make sense of the myriad issues we confront each day. Groups, therefore, provide individuals with a social reality, for they help to infuse meaning in situations that do not readily provide concrete explanations.

In their highly regarded text *Personal Influence*, Katz and Lazarsfeld (1955) suggest that individuals have specific identity groups in mind when forming opinions and rendering judgments about social practices. In time, individual identities become part of a larger group, and group members begin to interpret the world from a similar vantage as other members, thereby creating both group norms and a group-specific social reality.

Social groups, however, are not passive entities. As groups form upon a basis of mutual wants and needs, individuals have a vested interest in marketing group norms and ideals to recruit new members, to build internal solidarity, and to ensure the future existence of the collective. Groups, therefore, do not simply construct reality; they also promote it through a process of interpretive framing. A "frame" is a conceptualization that provides meaning to events. Every public event is subject to numerous interpretations regarding its cause, motive, and impact. Frames provide the context through which events are viewed, interpreted and critiqued. An idea developed by Goffman (1974) as an addendum of sorts to his symbolic metaphor of social life (Goffman, 1959), "framing" has become central to the constructionist paradigm. It asserts that groups use interpretive frames to simplify events by affixing meanings to situations that conform to previously established or understood group realities.

Merging the social with the political, Edelman (1975) argues that — like group behavior — government activity is predominantly symbolic. For Edelman, individuals and groups form opinions about the relative strength of society based not upon what representatives are actually doing but instead upon the emotions evoked by their varied symbolic activities, such as flag waving, the signing of a bill, or Congressional pomp and circumstance. Each day, various social groups — including political parties, lobbyists, policy think tanks, and non-government organizations — use the political arena to promote their own interpretation of reality, employing both symbols and gestures and applying interpretive frames to various political events. Politics, then, can be seen as "a passing parade of abstract symbols" (p.5) planted in the political spotlight by various groups and displayed by broadcast news, daily newspapers, and, of course, the political leaders themselves to construct impressions favorable to their group interests, thus carrying out the basic tenets of the constructionist paradigm.

Figure 1.

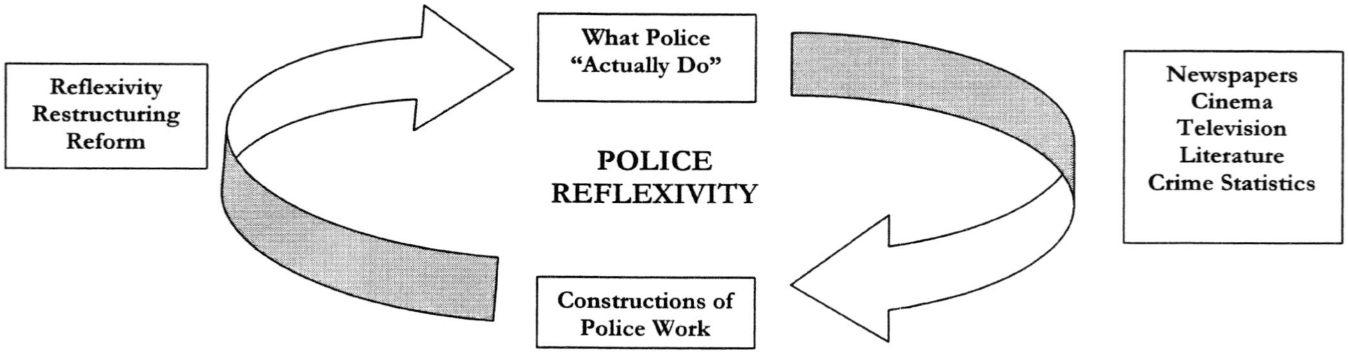

Newspapers
Cinema
Television
Literature
Crime Statistics

What Police
"Actually Do"

POLICE
REFLEXIVITY

Constructions of
Police Work

Reflexivity
Restructuring
Reform

But if reality is merely a social construct, then there is nothing inherently objective in the interpretation of these symbols. As Edelman (1975:11-13) notes:

> The meanings...are not in the symbols. They are in society and therefore in men...There is nothing about any symbol that requires that it stand for only one thing...For the spectators of the political scene every [symbol] contributes to a pattern of ongoing events that spells threat or reassurance. This is the basic dichotomy for the mass public...[T]hey will fit nicely as evidence to support people's preconceived hopes and fears.

Reality, then, is not only constructed through symbols and gestures, it is also contested, since there is no guarantee that individuals will come to share an interpretation of the symbolic meanings of these social and political performances. It is not uncommon to witness a Sunday morning talk show featuring two pundits with differing perceptions of recent political performances. In fact, as society becomes increasingly diverse, political and social fragmentation into numerous groups increases the number of claims into the "true" nature of these performances (Loseke, 1999). When this happens, the symbols that were once part of a shared collective become part of a political dichotomy debated and interpreted in the headlines of daily newspapers and through the flickering images on a screen.

Policing as a Contested Reality

Policing is among the most symbolic of all political functions, and certainly it is among the most contested. As an expression of the will of the State, its daily practice serves to reinforce the status quo, including its rules, norms, and values. It communicates the "awesome power that lies at the root of the political order" (Manning, 1997:21), as well as the ability of the State to exercise that power when the social order is threatened. The ceremony and ritual that comprises much of policing works to reinforce the tenets of tradition and commitment, while the tools that assist in creating these symbolic performances — such as published crime statistics — provide the public with insight into the relative health of the social order (see Figure 1).

Even on a more concrete level, the day-to-day strategies that comprise much of police work are similarly rooted in symbols. For decades, the "professional model" of American policing was based upon the notion that the mere presence of an officer in public places served as an effective deterrent to crime. The goal was to symbolically create the impression of a strong, omnipresent police force through the deployment of uniformed cops patrolling in marked vehicles. More style than substance, this strategy of policing has been described as primarily a matter of drama designed to maintain the public belief in the police as guardians of the social order (Manning, 1997:212).

Indeed, much of deterrence-based policing rests upon a phantom effect, or a belief in the presence of things that are not necessarily present (Walker and Katz, 2002). O.W. Wilson, a leading proponent of police patrol, explained that patrol is designed to create "an impression of omnipresence" that will eliminate the actual opportunity or the belief that the opportunity exists for successful misconduct (Wilson, 1963:228). Beginning in the late 1970s, experimentation with foot patrols had as its objective a change in public perceptions of crime, while symbolically recasting the officer as at one with the public. Interestingly, while actual crime levels did not change as a result of foot patrol, citizen perceptions of the incidence of crime did change, as did their level of fear, with the public under the belief that community problems were on the decline (Police Foundation, 1981). The more recent "broken windows" model of policing (Wilson and Kelling, 1982; Kelling and Coles, 1996) calls for officers to target minor social problems, such as graffiti and abandoned buildings, to offset the illusion that more serious crimes lie afoot, as well as to curtail their development.

As a social group, the police organization provides its members with a sense of identity and reinforces a particular ideology. Although by no means a monolithic entity, police organizations are typically staffed by individuals having a shared sense of public morality and a desire to maintain and/or establish those norms as cultural practice through law enforcement (Westley, 1970). While individuals having a particular cognitive framework are naturally attracted to the police organization, the process of training, social isolation, and shared occupational experiences serves to reinforce a particular construction of reality (Balch, 1972; Kappeler et al., 1998). In time, police officers begin to view the world through a similar cognitive lens (Skolnick, 1975), and they form a specific group norm as they continue to interact with each other relative to a common mission (Katz and Lazarsfeld, 1955).

Police, too, have a vested interest in presenting or, as is more often the case, withholding certain interpretations of reality to assure the public that they are maintaining order. Yet the very nature of police work and its dependence upon officer discretion all but ensures that police activities will receive much scrutiny and will be the subject of multiple interpretations by both insiders and, more importantly for the legitimacy of policing, by those operating outside of the police organization who will call police practices into question (Reiss, 1971). For this reason, police departments traditionally operate under a veil of secrecy. In an effort to present the appearance of order (Manning, 1997), police agencies deny outsiders access to their work environment for the purpose of impression management, thereby decreasing the amount of information available to the public that might point to either dirty or potentially illegal aspects of police work.

A central aspect of contemporary policing, then, involves the symbolic construction of law and order through the strategic use of officers, squad cars, and other occupational accouterments, as well as the deliberate framing of events in a manner that comports with the police ideology. Officers typically carry out the social construction of law and order by wearing the police badge as a symbol of honor and piety, by appearing and speaking in a professional and disciplined manner, and by donning the police uniform, which suggests that the individual is committed to upholding the principles of a larger collective. The police organization maintains the appearance of control through the staging of police practices such as routine preventive patrol, through concern displayed about rapid responses to calls for service, and through acquisition and use of cutting edge crime-fighting technology, all the while concealing that which undermines the organization's legitimacy.

But the police do not have a stranglehold on the interpretation of crime and justice events, nor on the use of symbolism in constructing meanings of law and order. Despite attempts by police and their lawyers to frame events as involving the use of "appropriate" levels of force (Shuster and Gorman, 2002), both the Rodney King and Donovan Jackson beatings became emblematic of widespread racism within law enforcement. Therefore, what to some appears to be the legitimate use of force will to others be emblematic of a force out-of-control; a cop on every corner may provide some citizens with comfort, others with unease. The symbols of policing are simply part of the basic dichotomy that supports people's preconceived hopes and fears, with police work a part of a broader process of construction and contention, of definition and debate.

This, however, does not imply that there are no police actions that, taken at face value, are either lawful or an overextension of power. It merely suggests that police practices, like all social behavior, are subject to multiple interpretations based upon the nature of the symbolic inter-action and the social context in which it arises. Police do not have a mo-nopoly on the interpretation of reality as it relates to law and order. Rather, they are merely one social and/or political group that is part of a daily struggle to maintain ownership over the symbolic definitions of social events and over the social construction of reality, a struggle that often places them at odds with other social and political groups, includ-ing the mass media.

Media's "Passing Parade of Abstract Symbols"

Like the police officers who collectively work to construct interpre-tations of their occupational practices, news reporters (and even Holly-wood scriptwriters) work to transform isolated and short-lived events into broader, more meaningful cultural narratives. As second-party sto-rytellers, journalists provide interpretive frames to the events they re-port, transforming slices of life into broader, more meaningful news items. Gamson and Modigliani (1989) argue that reporters apply a set of interpretive packages that contain a range of positions on various issues, with each frame presenting themes for the purpose of a broader social metaphor. Jones (1993) notes that news stories most typically revolve around one of the compelling "C's": catastrophe, crisis, conflict, crime, corruption, and color (i.e., human interest). Lule (2001) suggests that news frames conform to one of many enduring cultural archetypes and that a news story is essentially that: a story that draws upon mythical sta-ples in an attempt to interpret or make sense of the world.

One of the functions of mass media, therefore, and in particular the news media, is to provide the public with an interpretation of events that is above and beyond the mere dissemination of "facts." Whether one adheres to the Durkheimian model of society where the criminal vic-timization of one individual is symbolic of the victimization of the col-lective, or instead to a more conflict-based interpretation of society where victimization is symbolic of social and/or economic imbalances, few topics are more culturally meaningful to the body politic than crime and its control. The inherent symbolism of criminal victimization provides one explanation as to why crime narratives are regular and daily features in the news. As one reporter explained:

> What I look for are stories that are interesting at face value, but also on a deeper level. What does this story say about who we are as a city? Who we are as a people? As white people? As black people? Stories that can be used as metaphors for something bigger. Obviously, not all crime stories are that. Most of them aren't...But I do think you see more of those [metaphoric] stories in crime stories than [in], say, a city council meeting (Lovell, 2001).

This storytelling function places the media as key figures in the social construction of events, and with crime so prominently featured in mass media, police activities are susceptible to media constructions and conflicting interpretations, for even isolated police activities are always symbolic of something bigger. Newspapers, movies, television programs, even children's comic books, therefore, represent a terrain of ideological struggle where the constructions of justice are formed and debated. Typically, government officials have an advantage in this struggle over media content since reporters and entertainers are dependent upon these sources of cooperation for story assistance. As a result, law enforcement has been actively involved in the creation of some of the most popular police personas, including Sergeant Joe Friday of television's *Dragnet* and Special Agent Clarice Starling of the movie *The Silence of the Lambs*.

Nevertheless, police often feel at a disadvantage in the construction of reality when the images are of real events. They often feel that the news media have a bias against them (Reiner, 1992). A survey of 200 police officers conducted by Niederhoffer (1969:234) revealed that 95% of respondents felt that newspapers "seem to enjoy giving an unfavorable slant to news concerning the police." Police also feel that members of the news media have a misunderstanding of the role of law enforcement in society (Ziembo-Vogl, 1998), sensationalize violent crime incidents, and fail to assess organizational and budgetary constraints when reporting on the police (Skolnick and McCoy, 1984). Moreover, in the words of Hubert Williams, former chief of the Newark Police Department and now head of the Police Foundation, "the media's mistake is to look at events, not a progression of events" (quoted in Skolnick and McCoy, 1984:543).

The inability of police to maintain control over the interpretation of events is compounded when new forms of media technology are introduced into society. New media provide the public with new information, leading to new characterizations and to new interpretations of police work. They permeate the aural and visual boundaries that once concealed many aspects of police behavior. Whereas the police may try to shield many of their activities from public view, new media, and especially the electronic media, penetrate the shield of police secrecy, potentially threatening the legitimacy of the persona that the police have so carefully constructed. The intrusiveness and expanding pervasiveness of mass media, then, makes the construction of a favorable public persona increasingly difficult for the police to achieve. With each new advancement in media technology, it becomes exceedingly difficult for police to proactively present a construction of events. Increasingly caught off guard, police now find themselves attempting to repair a damaged public image and engaging in the reactive construction of a public image.

In response to new media technology, time and again the police have had to restructure their performance according to the requirements of evolving media technology for the purpose of maintaining their aura of legitimacy. Such restructuring of behavior based upon mediated images represents a practice of performance reflexivity, where mass media serve as an important source of information regarding popular interpretations of police work. Subsequent chapters will provide the reader with examples of how evolving police practices have — in part — been fashioned in response to new image-producing technology and the new interpretations of police work they provide to the public. But first, a more thorough understanding of the ways media contribute to reflexivity and the construction of reality is in order.

NOTES

1. Quoted from a confidential, internal department memorandum obtained as part of a larger study on police-media relations nationwide (NIJ# 2000-IJ-CX-0046). The study is hereafter cited as Lovell, 2001.

2. MEDIA AND REFLEXIVITY

"The sun is mirrored even in a coffee spoon."
Siegfried Giedion[1]

A rather curious observation from a scholar of history, Giedion's (1955) comment firmly establishes the extent to which society has come to resemble a magical mirror. Indeed, one of the defining features of modern times is our ability to alter the social environment based upon the many reflections that we receive. A by-product of the information age, virtually every facet of daily life is now monitored for the purpose of revision and improvement. Birth, marriage, divorce, employment, air quality, currency, mortality, census data and crime statistics are all part of a massive feedback loop that defines and refines who we are as a people and how we progress as a society, and they all contribute to a process known as cultural reflexivity. Reflexivity occurs when we use the information contained in this feedback loop to alter our cultural patterns and to reform our social conduct.

The concept of cultural reflexivity rests upon two key assumptions. First, it assumes that people and organizations use information for instrumental (i.e., goal-oriented) purposes. Information about the self and our surroundings triggers a set of behavioral responses that causes either a revision or reinforcement of cultural patterns. The goal is to use information for the improvement or refinement of social behavior. This implies, however, that individuals do not consume information passively but instead use information rather actively when it pertains to the self or to the immediate surrounding. Specifically, Potter (1996) suggests that in the daily construction of behavior, what begins as descriptive information ultimately becomes incorporated into the very object being described, for rarely is information about the self treated as abstract and disembodied. More likely, information contributes either to action or a deliberate inaction that, upon reflection, produces even more descriptive information. As Potter summarizes, information "is both *about* some piece of interaction and also a contribution *to* that interaction; that is, it is reflexive" (p. 49).

A second notion of reflexivity assumes that individuals and organizations are — more or less — rational entities that use information to maximize opportunities. According to rational choice theory, information is an important tool necessary to the attainment of benefits, for information provides social actors with insight regarding how best to cater their performance to achieve a satisfactory outcome. Under the rational choice model, then, reflexivity is essential for the success of personal and professional goals. That is, in the daily activities of personal and professional life, cultural reflexivity proves central to cost-benefit analysis that guides social and administrative behavior.

Yet as even the most casual observers of social and administrative behavior are aware, individuals and groups often suffer from what Simon (1976) refers to as an acute case of rational "schizophrenia." We are all familiar with instances where people give in to group pressure against their better judgment or simply behave in a manner that — upon reflection — was probably not the most rational of available options. Indeed, according to more social psychological models of human behavior, people behaving in groups settings are not nearly as rational as the theory of rational choice would have us believe (Asch, 1958; Milgram, 1974). Not merely an academic argument, the extent to which social actors behave in a deliberate manner is pivotal to the premise of cultural reflexivity and to the potential for personal and professional change. After all, theories of symbolic interaction and social construction are predicated upon the assertion that information garnered from social cues provides a sense of self, and that behavioral patterns are both a product of and reaction to this social information, resulting in a reflexive feedback loop. But if rationality does not, in fact, guide group behavior, then the ability of external cues to exert pressure for reform becomes improbable, as does the possibility that police — who necessarily conform to group norms — routinely engage in cultural reflexivity.

In line with conventional wisdom on the limits of rational choice theory, Simon (1976) presents a model of "intendedly" rational behavior that guides administrative behavior and that helps to qualify the argument postulating a cycle of police reflexivity and organizational reform. The reader will recall from the Introduction that arguments postulating police organizational immutability are mere myth. That is, the police organization has undergone several measurable changes since its formal emergence during the mid-nineteenth century. At the same time, the police organization — like all bureaucracies — does not readily lend itself to expedient and dramatic change. Instead, the process is often quite slow and frequently met with resistance.

Discussing the decision-making processes of large organizations, Simon provides two crucial explanations as to why bureaucracies are less rational, and therefore, less thoroughly reflexive, than individuals. First, whereas individuals seek to maximize opportunities by selecting the best option, bureaucracies often must choose a course of action that is merely "good enough." That is, administrators seek to take the course of action necessary for change, but they don't want to bring about so much change as to disrupt the overall structure or functioning of the organization. Secondly, whereas individuals function in a far broader and arguably more complex environment, organizations function in a more limited capacity, hence administrators make decisions based upon a more simplified picture of the environment and with limited reflection.

All of this is meant to qualify the rather bold assertion that police organizations are amenable to change from external and often critical sources, such as the media. Police organizations tend to be marked by a subculture that is rather distinct from that culture of the civilian population (Skolnick, 1975), and they tend to feel that outsiders, especially the media, have a misunderstanding of the dynamics of that culture and of the role of law enforcement in society (Ziembo-Vogl, 1998). Nevertheless, it is increasingly difficult to maintain assertions that the police are resistant to pressure from the media for change. Whether or not their actions are misunderstood, the mass media convert police events into a central part of our common culture, a culture that both shapes and is shaped by police activities. And the history of law enforcement is replete with examples of police engagement in cultural reflexivity.

From the very first scandalous headlines that appeared in the penny press, damage control became a central component of effective police leadership. Traditionally, police would try to avoid media coverage outright, opting instead to work silently and behind the scenes to repair a tarnished image. Today, many police departments actively seek out media coverage of their activities (e.g., TV's *Real Stories of the Highway Patrol*, *COPs*) for the purpose of shaping and reshaping cultural attitudes toward police behavior, attitudes that will — in turn — reinforce or re-legitimate police practices. Police also have a keen sense of their image as portrayed in popular culture. As will become apparent in the chapters that follow, police often endorse Hollywood productions that seize upon the "good cop" aspects of the popular imagination while working feverishly to denounce those that focus upon the "bad cop" aspects of the police image.

The media have also been a force for police cultural reflexivity in more tangible or measurable ways. Police periodically revise their crime control strategies (whether in the short or long run) following intense media scrutiny of police tactics. Examples have included reexaminations of the controversial police choke hold (Fisher, 1993), police involvement in high-speed hot pursuits (Ortega, 1992; Fine, 1999; Garza, 2003), and the use of pepper spray to apprehend or subdue suspects (Schwennesen, 2000). And they engage in cultural reflexivity when they allow criminal justice researchers access to their facilities and staff for the purpose of evaluating new police policies that were often put into practice as a result of intense media and public debate.

Thus, law enforcement agencies routinely engage in cultural reflexivity, and the media represent a powerful source of police organizational change. Moreover, as information technology continues to expand at an rapid pace, it follows that police will continue to become increasingly dependent upon the mass media for evaluations of police performance as well as indications of the level of public support for current police practices. Yet the implications of an increasing police dependency upon mass media for performance cues are by no means trivial. After all, the media are filled with exaggerated and competing claims about the successes and failures of police performance, and they are filled with competing and contradictory assertions regarding the political acceptability of the maverick, rogue cop. This chapter concludes with a more comprehensive discussion of the images and realities of contemporary police work in contemporary media. First, a discussion of the role of mass media on socialization and social interaction is in order.

MASS MEDIA AND SOCIALIZATION

The previous chapter noted that cultural patterns arise in large part through a process of social interaction. Introducing the constructionist paradigm, it explained the formation of social norms as part of a practice of symbolic communication through which individuals form definitions about themselves, their surroundings, and the acceptability of their daily activities through a series of face-to-face communications. These communications function as a means of behavioral reinforcement where individual actions are deemed as either acceptable or inappropriate through largely non-verbal communications, such as direct eye contact, physical gestures, and other forms of body language and group behavior. Daily and face-to-face interaction with others, therefore, is basic to the formation of social norms, for it is in the presence of an audience that individuals receive cues as to the strength of their everyday performances.

When a new technology enters an environment, however, it necessarily alters the nature of its social organization. One of the consequences of mass media is that social interaction becomes less necessary and, therefore, less frequent. Theorists such as Karl Marx (1844 [1988]), Emile Durkheim (1951 [1979]) and Max Weber (1958) documented how technology reshapes the patterns of production and contribute to economic and political alienation. More contemporary theorists (Meyrowitz, 1986) have noted a rise in individualism and social alienation brought about by media technology. However examined, the decline in face-to-face encounters in favor of mediated experiences represents one of the more notable consequences of technological innovation (DeFleur and Ball-Rokeach, 1989; Croteau and Hoynes, 2000).

But if meaning has traditionally derived through a process of social interaction, then the growth of a new, technology-driven society ensures that thought processes and behavioral patterns will be molded in response to the mediated interaction that now replaces face-to-face communication. In this new era, realities are no longer constructed through cumulative and lived experiences but are instead constructed in response to the media messages that have become the new source of reflexive monitoring. With the bulk of our daily information stemming from newspapers, the television, books and movies, we are today increasingly dependent upon mass media for the symbols and cues that provide us with an understanding of who we are, how we should behave socially, and when necessary, how we should reform our current social practices. In short, we are increasingly dependent upon mass media as a source of socialization.

Socialization is the process whereby we learn and internalize the values, beliefs, and norms of our culture. It is through socialization that we discover the limits of acceptable and unacceptable social practices and gain a broad understanding of cultural expectations. For years, schools, churches, and the family have played a key role in providing us with the information necessary to make sense of the world. Today, mass media represent a primary socializing agent, especially given their expanding importance in everyday life (Croteau and Hoynes, 2000). Educators increasingly rely upon media for assistance when planning daily curricula, and parents have come to trust the television as a last resort for occupying the attention of a rambunctious child. It has been estimated that by the time the average child graduates from high school s/he will have spent more time in front of the television than in the classroom (Graber, 1997). Adults, too, are socialized by media messages. They turn to the newspapers and television to learn about political norms, the economy, family life and dating practices, and they fashion their behavior based upon the messages they receive from self-help books, the stock pages, even paid advertisements. Hour after hour, various aspects of society are repeatedly presented to the public in a similar manner, increasing the possibility that these values and norms will become part of the audience's cognitive framework.

It is important to note that as agents of socialization, the mass media are neither politically nor culturally neutral. Like the cultural definitions and meanings that are communicated through direct social interaction, media messages are inherently ideological in that they suggest a normative mode of behavior. They define social practices and normalize social relations such as gender roles, race relations, even the practice of law and order (Croteau and Hoynes, 2000). While no individual is likely to be swayed by all media messages, factors such as the relevance of the message to the recipient, the credibility of the source, and the attitudinal predisposition of the audience contribute to the likelihood that the media messages will influence audience cognition and/or behavior (Petty and Priester, 1994; Jo and Berkowitz, 1994). This may prove especially problematic when repeated images appear to normalize extraordinary social behaviors.

Since the emergence of television on the American scene during the 1950s, the U.S. government has conducted numerous investigations in an attempt to measure the extent to which media may normalize various social patterns. Both the Surgeon General's Scientific Advisory Committee on Television and Social Behavior (1972) and the National Institute of Mental Health's summary report (1982) concluded that media could elicit some forms of behavior in some viewers. Specifically, these government investigations concluded that visual violence could contribute to the development of aggressive behavior in the disposition of young television viewers (Surette, 1998). But where the government inquiries were rather limited in scope and focused exclusively upon visual violence, other studies have linked media to the socialization of specific attitudes about gender (Donnerstein et al., 1987), the trustworthiness of neighbors (Gerbner and Gross, 1976), support for various crime control policies (Barille, 1984), and to high levels of fear and unease (Chiricos, 1998).

While most researchers agree that media represent key agents in the process of socialization, there is less agreement upon the relative contribution of media to individual or cultural patterns. Many theories argue that the mass media have the ability to inject messages into the bloodstream of the public — the hypodermic model — thereby directly influencing both behavior and public opinion (Lasswell, 1927; see also Katz and Lazarsfeld, 1954 for a discussion). Other models suggest that the media's impact on audiences is weak and short-lived. This "minimal-effects" approach to understanding media promotes the idea that media might merely reinforce pre-existing beliefs among viewers (Lazarsfeld et al., 1968). Finally, the agenda-setting hypothesis (McCombs and Shaw, 1972) stands at a theoretical middle ground, claiming that media have the ability to direct the public's attention toward certain political and social issues through their shaping of news headlines and content (Croteau and Hoynes, 2000).

Whether one adheres to a determinist model of mass media or to a more conservative stance of minimal effects, what should by now be clear is that, at the very least, media messages have an ability to contribute to the formation of attitudes and opinions, and under some circumstances, even contribute to behavior, though the exact nature of the relationship may be difficult to determine. Symbolic interaction theorist Herbert Blumer (1986) makes the following suggestions to researchers interested in understanding the role of mass media in the process of socialization: because the content of media is by no means homogeneous, the identification of a specific content of media for investigation is necessary; because the composition of the audience is similarly diverse, the identification of sensitive audiences for whom the messages are relevant is similarly necessary; finally, an effort should be made to determine the political or social context contributing to audience sensitivity toward specific media messages. Any given media influence should be studied in relation to other influences which may be operating in the area of concern.

With such methodological ground rules in play, one can begin to ascertain the influence of mass media in establishing social norms more generally, and in influencing police performance more specifically. The remainder of this chapter focuses upon a specific content of media imagery, namely, those images of the police and of contemporary policing. Specifically, it examines ideological consistencies in the portrayal of the police persona and in the dynamics of police work. It then turns its attention to the audience members who are likely to be the most sensitive to popular images of law enforcement: the police. While most investigations into media effects focus upon children as the audience members most susceptible to media socialization, with police among the most featured professions in mass media, one would expect that images of policing in popular culture will have special meaning to those engaged in the daily responsibility of law enforcement and will contribute to the reflexive monitoring of police practices.

IMAGES AND REALITIES OF POLICE WORK

Images of dramatic shoot-outs and sensational crime fighting occupy a prominent place in the mainstream of popular culture. Since the early days of mass media, detective stories, the murder mystery, and the hard-boiled "private eye" have delivered to the public a unique brand of law and order that continues to glamorize the investigative and crime-fighting aspects of police work. On the small screen, television cops apprehend criminals in daredevil fashion, never failing to bring about a complete resolution to the day's events. In Hollywood, big budgets and explosive special effects drape law enforcement in a blanket of fantasy where car chases, gun slinging, and violent confrontations are essential to bringing about justice.

Such is the world of make-believe, where police work is synonymous with crime fighting, and crime fighting is by and large a successful endeavor. In the real world, however, police seldom perform as crime fighters. Instead, they spend most of their time providing citizens with service-oriented assistance (Mastrofski, 1983). When police do perform in their capacity as crime fighters, they are seldom as successful as their popular image suggests. In fact, official crime statistics suggest that the police are successful in solving only 21% of all reported "Index" offenses,[2] though their success rate for clearing the specifically violent offenses most likely to be dramatized by media is much higher (Walker and Katz, 2002). The public typically does not herald the police as heroes either. Rather, the police role is one marked by suspicion and skepticism, where officers are charged with the contradictory task of policing an ostensibly free society (Goldstein, 1977).

Despite the popularity of the superhero cop, characterizations of real-world police periodically find their way into the popular culture mainstream and provide the public a source of ridicule and commentary on police ineptitude. The Keystone Kops of the early twentieth century have become emblematic of police inefficiency by being both underfunded and under-educated. Chief Clancy Wiggum of television's *The Simpsons* is likely to be seen pursuing the wrong suspect or consuming large amounts of junk food that causes him immediate shortness of breath and an inability to perform "real" police work. The news media, too, have disseminated their share of negative police imagery. Videotaped footage of the beating of motorist Rodney King, the discovery during the O.J. Simpson trial of L.A. detective Mark Furhman's racist remarks, and the more recent incidents of the shootings of unarmed men by the New York and Cincinnati Police Departments are all part of the diverse media imagery that define who the police are and how they should perform their duties.

Today, both the positive and negative media images of police work compete for the public's attention and serve as the backdrop against which everyday police practices are evaluated and assessed. The result in the creation of a good cop/bad cop dichotomy of media imagery in whose shadow the police must operate. On the one hand, fictional images of the police as crime fighter present the public with an *ideal* of police work, the "good" cop. But because these images are grounded in fiction and fantasy, the "good" cop is merely an ideal that is unlikely to ever be reached. On the other hand are images of equally extreme police behavior that are found primarily in the news media, but also in such

Keystone-esque caricatures that expose acts of police abuse, malfeasance, or inefficiency. These images all contribute to demands for bringing about reform and a change to this style of "bad" cop policing.

Haunted by this specter of media imagery, the police find it difficult to position themselves publicly in the middle ground between the unattainable fictional and the unfortunate factual. To be sure, police aspire to be the fictional "good" cop, as they have come to define police work in a manner that resembles the work of their fictional counterparts. Eschewing the mundane aspects of everyday policing, they suggest that crime fighting constitutes "real" police work, while they refer to the more community, service-oriented aspect of their job pejoratively as social work (Perlmutter, 2000). The public, too, has by and large bought into the mediated ideal of crime and justice through their support of 100,000 more police on the streets as the most effective and practical means of reducing crime, while additional and/or alternative means of crime reduction (e.g., midnight basketball or funding for social programs) are met with cynicism and concerns over wasteful spending (Weisskopf, 1994; Gest, 2001). Yet adherence to a fictional ideal can prove problematic, and with regard to policing, there is no greater fiction than the media version of a good cop.

Good Cop

The good cop stands as one of the most popular characters in contemporary fiction and has become an essential feature of the crime *genre*. A genre represents a category of art where themes, characters, and situations become familiar to audiences and perpetuate a given structure or format. Examples include the western, the horror, and the science fiction genres. At its core, the crime genre works in terms of transgression and retribution (Clarens, 1997), with the good cop playing an essential role in converting the former into the latter. Ironically, the good cop is defined not by his adherence to legal norms but by his *effectiveness*, as the good cop is frequently a rogue or "dirty" officer who resorts to extra-legal techniques in the pursuit of law and order. Moreover, the good cop is not defined by his employment in a conventional law enforcement agency but instead by his indefatigable pursuit of justice. The good cop may be a detective or a private investigator, a maverick or an officer turned outsider. Whoever he is, he is always successful.

The popularity of the good cop stems from the fact that his activities are emblematic of so many cultural expectations and aspirations. On one level, his meticulous scrutiny of even minor evidentiary details represents the embodiment of Enlightenment ideals, where science and reason prove effective in solving human problems. These ideals helped popularize the detective novels of Edgar Allan Poe and Sir Arthur Conan Doyle at the height of industrial progress (Thompson, 1993), and they likely explain the recent popularity of such TV programs as *Law and Order* and *CSI*. On another level, the good cop's technocratic and managerial style represents a pragmatic solution to crime and deviance (e.g., television's *Dragnet*), yet the occasional circumvention of legal constraints evident in the rogue cop (e.g., *Dirty Harry*) promotes individualism and restores a sense of street credibility to law enforcement (Buxton, 1990). The good cop also reinforces ideas of masculinity in contemporary society (Rafter, 2000), as the good cop always knows where and when to "shoot his gun." Finally, the good cop connotes a sense of morality, restoring peace and tranquility to a fallen world (Buxton, 1990) plagued by drugs and prostitution (e.g., the TV show *Miami Vice*).

In sum, where the typical police department may be struggling to define its priorities in terms of law enforcement, order maintenance, and community service — a struggle that may limit what police can accomplish (Perez, 1997) — the goals of the good cop are presented as frighteningly simplistic. Where policing in a free society requires strict adherence to bureaucratic, legal and constitutional constraints, the media good cop is free from such legal handcuffs and constitutional shackles. And where police discretion is subject to intense public scrutiny and the use of force is relegated to a last resort, strength and autonomy from all oversight are key defining features of the good cop.

Bad Cop

Media images of the "bad" cop tap into our cultural fears of a society at the brink of lawlessness and chaos. Comprised of both fictional and non-fictional imagery, the bad cop represents the failures of our justice system and reminds us that more often than not, crime does in fact pay. In fiction, the bad cop is often a caricature of an unskilled and uneducated detective who is perhaps the last person that should be armed with a gun (e.g., the movies *Police Academy* and *The Naked Gun*). But he may also be personified as morally corrupt and the very antithesis of what we expect from law enforcement (e.g., the movies *Bad Lieutenant* and *Training Day*). In real life, the bad cop may not be too different from these characterizations. The Wickersham Commission reports published in 1931 exposed police corruption and inefficiency among police of that era (National Commission on Law Observance and Enforcement, 1931 [1968]). Four decades later, the Knapp Commission exposed widespread corruption within the New York Police Department (Knapp Commission, 1973). More recently, a Los Angeles Police Department Board of Inquiry investigated allegations of corruption on the part of officers assigned to the Rampart area (Parks, 2000).

In addition to these facts, it is important to note that the mere presence of the fictional "good" cop on the cultural landscape can create the appearance of the real life "bad" cop simply because the typical officer cannot possibly achieve the level of success attained by his fictional counterpart. In the same manner that the typical middle-class family appears wholly dysfunctional and ill equipped to raise children when compared to TV's *The Cosby Show* or *The Brady Bunch*, in terms of imagery alone the typical urban police department appears ill equipped to carry out its public mandate when compared to television's *T.J. Hooker* or *NYPD Blue*.

Thus, whereas the good cop's mandate is irreducibly that of the crime fighter, everyday police work is multi-faceted, involving elements of order maintenance, community service, and preventive patrol. Whereas audiences express little outrage at the extra-legal measures adopted by "dirty" Harry or Andy Sipowicz, the officers who staff the nation's police departments do not have the luxury of operating outside of the law. They are "constrained" (and rightfully so) by numerous legal, political, and ethical pressures that fail to encumber the media's rogue crime fighter. And whereas the fictional cop can single-handedly bring about a complete resolution to the most baffling case, real-life detective work requires many hours of teamwork and extensive financial resources.

In sum, the bad cop represents the polar opposite of the fictional good cop. He is unskilled, uneducated, and inept. He is not beneath accepting bribes or perjuring himself on the stand. But unlike the good cop, who pursues extra-legal means for altruistic ends, the bad cop is driven by self-promotion. At the same time, because the public has come to define police work in terms of crime fighting and risk taking, in light of the successes of the good cop the real cop appears less than effective, less than efficient, and at times, less than capable of solving even the most mundane of crimes. Standing side by side with his heroic media brethren, today's real cop is often branded as at best mediocre and at worst as nothing less than simply a "bad" cop.

The "Hyperreal"

The trappings of the good cop/bad cop dichotomy are best understood when examined within the framework of a postmodern analysis. While the complexities of postmodernism are beyond the scope of this book and are by no means universally accepted, theorists examining the question of epistemology at the end of the nineteenth and throughout the twentieth century have come to appreciate the centrality of mass media in both defining and shaping our collective sense of "reality." Increasingly, human knowledge and cognition is traceable not to an original, tangible or even real source, but instead to its simulated representation as featured in the images of the mass media (Baudrillard, 1983). One of the central features of postmodernity, then, is the prominence of mediated experience in our daily lives. No longer do we encounter reality firsthand; instead, much of the information that shapes our conception of society is filtered through some form of media (Anderson, 1990; Lyotard, 1997).

That worldly events are increasingly experienced only second-hand has tremendous consequences for our understanding of reality. For example, most citizens experience war not by engaging in battle, but by responding to the horrific imagery featured in such motion pictures as *Saving Private Ryan,* which was billed as "the most realistic" portrayal of the horrors of war to date. But without experiencing war first hand, in time these representations of war become the basis upon which we assess the true horrors of war, rather than the other way around. That is, should a war actually break out, and should its images be carried on CNN (which, again, is still one degree removed from "reality"), it is likely that we will assess the realism and shock of what we see on CNN based upon its fictional (i.e., *Saving Private Ryan*) representation. When conditions occur wherein reality is assessed according to its representation, we have entered the realm of the postmodern where the prominence of reality has given way to its media imagery.

A postmodern critique of contemporary culture therefore asserts that images of reality are often (mis)taken for reality itself. Perhaps no other cultural critique has summarized this postmodern (i.e., post-Enlightenment) trend better than Jean Baudrillard (1983), who describes contemporary culture as the age of the "hyperreal." The hyperreal is not in fact reality but rather a representation designed to elucidate or mediate aspects of our cultural climate. Problems arise, however, when individuals respond as strongly (or stronger) to these mediated representations as they do to the very reality they were designed to represent. A condition of hyperreality is said to occur when individuals no longer respond directly to reality but only to its mediated representation.

Baudrillard identifies the iconoclasts as being the first individuals appropriately cautious of the harm to our epistemological sensibilities that could result from the dominance of representational images and simulated reality. It was the iconoclasts, says Baudrillard, who sensed the omnipresence and subsequent rise in the status of the representation at the expense and devaluation of the real. They foresaw the problem of venerating God "at one remove" as ultimately leading to the virtual disappearance of God, or what he refers to contemporarily as the death of the real. Writing metaphorically, Baudrillard (1996) notes that the murder of reality constitutes "the perfect crime" because there is no identifiable criminal, no tangible victim, and no apparent motive. Simply put, with reality the murder victim, there remains no traceable corpse, and with representations already replacing the real, the crime remains largely undetected.

Far from hyperbole or exaggeration, there are many everyday examples of the death of the real, or what others have referred to in less dramatic jargon as the merging of fiction and reality. It is not uncommon for television actors to be mistaken for the characters they portray (Best and Kellner, 1991). During his tenure as television's Dr. Marcus Welby, actor Robert Young received thousands of letters from the public requesting medical advice. Capitalizing on his hyperreal status, he later appeared in advertisements promoting the safety of decaffeinated coffee to individual health. Of course, it was up to the consumer to decide if it was Young or his fictional counterpart who was promoting the product. Similarly, both Raymond Burr and — more recently — Calista Flockhart received requests for legal assistance as a result of their respective TV portrayals of *Perry Mason* and *Ally McBeal*. And actors portraying villainous soap opera characters have had to hire bodyguards when out in public to protect themselves.

Yet this mistake of fact is merely the beginning of what may become a never-ending reality-altering process, for hyperreality always exists within a broader climate that engages in cultural reflexivity. This means that simulations are not merely mistaken for reality, they also become the model upon which reality is based. To understand this, one need only examine the extent to which recent cultural trends have become symptomatic and reflective of widespread media imagery.

REFLEXIVE POLICING

Mass media provide the context in which culture is created, defined, and experienced. As individuals become increasingly isolated from direct social interaction, while they simultaneously become more dependent upon mediated experiences, the possibility becomes increasingly likely that we will begin to understand the "real" only in terms of its representation (Baudrillard, 1981; Charney and Schwartz, 1995). This becomes especially problematic for the police, as most citizens have little direct interaction with law enforcement but instead experience police symbolically through the "good" cop/"bad" cop media representations. Recognizing the ever-expanding importance of media imagery to the success of policing, officers and agencies are beginning to police their public image by monitoring the mass media and reforming their performance in a reflexive manner. Note the following example provided by a sergeant trained as a police-media specialist:

> The VCR/Camcorder is affecting how we do our job. Our city has a big festival every year. Last year I was working the event with some other officers when a man began causing trouble. He eventually became aggressive and resistant. Sometimes the only way to restrain a guy is to use physical force, which we began to do. Then, I noticed people in the gathering crowd filming the incident with their camcorders, and I immediately signaled 'cameras' to the other officers, imagining how it would appear on the local news. Because the public doesn't understand police proce-

dures, we ended up using less force and ultimately put ourselves in danger (Lovell, 2001).

Acutely aware of how things "would appear on the local news" and by proxy, in the mind of the public, theoretical or historical treatments of police practices can no longer understate the role of mass media in shaping the nature of police work. Officers themselves now recognize the importance of media imagery to successful policing, and we now know that they actively engage in the reflexive monitoring of their public performances and have done so following each advancement in media technology — the video camera being only the most recent innovation. What is unknown, however, is the extent of the media's influence on police practices relative to other social forces. On the one hand, given that political, social, and economic factors likely have a more direct impact upon police practices, the influence of imagery on contemporary policing is likely to adhere to the "minimal-effects" model of mass media. On the other hand, it is through media that the public discovers the effects of political, social and economic forces on police work, as well the consequences of police work for political, social, and economic forces.

One media effect that appears ever-present is the definition and/or reinforcement of the notion that police work connotes crime fighting. As an example, David Perlmutter (2000) spent nearly four years conducting ethnographic research of street cops in a small suburban police department with a relatively low crime rate. During this time, he rode with cops, observed their practices, communicated with them, and most importantly, photographed the officers for what he told them was a book about the nature of police work. While this was in fact true, he did not communicate with the officers his interest in the interaction of mediated policing and real-world policing.

Interestingly, Perlmutter found that throughout his period of observation officers would repeatedly recommend photo opportunities (e.g., "Here's a good shot;" "Have your camera ready") that captured the media stereotypes of police work, such as making an arrest, while photographs taken of the more common tasks of filing paper work or filling squad cars with gas at the pump were derided by officers out of fear that, "They'll think we're boring." At the conclusion of his lengthy study, Perlmutter allowed the officers to select copies of photographs that they could keep for themselves. Overwhelmingly, the officers selected those photographs that portrayed the kind of work they do as daring and dramatic. But as the author (p. 13) notes:

> It is not purely a case of cops thinking that they must look as people wanted them to look. They themselves — as evidenced by their comments...— have a love-hate relationship of a sort with their televisual and cinematic counterpart. They resent having to live up to him or her, but they have absorbed the value standard definition of cop herohood...Hence, the influences of indirectly mediated reality bounce back and forth in the echo chamber of culture and society.

It is, of course, the media generated "back and forth" that constitutes the "echo chamber" that is at the very essence of cultural reflexivity.

Another study of police-media reflexivity yielded rather disturbing results whose implications suggest that the media's tendency to generate definitions of police work might translate into actual police behavior. As part of a larger study into the attitudes and expectations of Miami police recruits, Surette (1995) noted that a controversial police shooting that occurred during the course of the study afforded an opportunity to test the effects of the subsequent media coverage on new recruit expectations. The incident involved the shooting and killing of a black motorcyclist by a Hispanic Miami officer in a predominantly black community. In the week following the event, the shooting was the focus of 53 newspaper stories and extensive television and radio coverage. To test for a possible media effect, police academy trainees were surveyed before and after academy training, during which time the shooting occurred. After controlling for an array of variables, Surette found that Hispanic recruits were more likely to report an expectation of weapon use during the course of police work after the shooting than they had prior to the incident. But while all of the recruits experienced a change in attitudes following training toward such topics as civil liberties, political cynicism, and trust in people, Hispanics represented the only group of recruits to undergo a change in weapon-use expectations.

Whether media representations of police work contribute to the formation of actual police practices was not within the scope of Surette's (1995) study, and no conclusions can be drawn about whether police are behaviorally susceptible to media imagery. Yet Surette does note that, "it is disturbing that the recruits' expectation of future gun use is revealed as highly volatile and subject to somewhat capricious external influences" (p. 363). Indeed. But concern that police behavior may be subject to external factors becomes even greater when one considers that many images of police practices are anything but capricious. While the exact nature of the media representation may fluctuate, the "good" cop/"bad" cop dichotomy remains a constant, leaving us to speculate on myriad other ways imagery might influence reality. Does "good" cop imagery raise public expectations of successful police work to unrealistic levels? Does it raise the expectations of new police recruits, who may reflexively alter their performance to adhere to this dramatic, risk-taking fictional ideal? In such a case, could "good cop" imagery contribute to "bad" cop policing, with officers more likely to fire a gun or circumvent police procedurals?

Uncovering the myriad ways mass media may influence police practices remains an important objective for media scholars and criminal justice researchers, though it is likely that we may never come to appreciate the full impact of mass media on social patterns. For as C. Wright Mills (1968:311) noted before the advent of video cameras, computers and the Internet, "...in their entirety these functions are probably so pervasive and so subtle that they cannot be caught by the means of social research now available." Nevertheless, in the pages that follow, I hope to illustrate some of the ways that new media technology, coupled with the new forms of information they disseminate, combine with political and social forces to create a so-called massive feedback loop, allowing for police officials and civic leaders to reflect upon the successes and failures of various police practices and reform their strategies based upon the mediated information they receive.

NOTES

1. Giedion, S. (1955).

2. "Index Crimes" are a composite of eight serious criminal offenses that are used to compute crime rates. These include: murder, forcible rape, robbery, aggravated assault, burglary, larceny-theft, motor vehicle theft, and arson.

3. *"READ ALL ABOUT IT!"*
POLICE AND THE PRESS

> *Neither political, constitutional, ecclesiastical, and economic events, nor sociological, philosophical and literary movements can be fully understood... without taking into account the influence the printing press has exerted upon them.*
> S. Steinberg[1]

On October 26, 1906, readers of the *New York Times* were presented with the following details, all couched under a headline declaring the "Biggest Shake-up in Police History:"

> Every police Captain of the greater city...was shifted yesterday. Most of them spent yesterday in packing their belongings and consulting maps to discover in what part of the five boroughs their lot was to be cast until it pleases the Commissioner to shake up the department again.

> Eighty-five Captains were transferred yesterday morning, and in eighty-five police stations last night eighty-five Sergeants were trying to explain to their new chiefs the exact nature of the new problems with which they would have to deal.

> It was the biggest police shake-up there has ever been in the New York police force...

> To the reporters the Commissioner vouchsafed very little in the way of explanation of the transfers, but he did intimate that there were more to come.

> ...At Police Headquarters and at Tammany Hall the transfers were attributed to politics.[2]

Referred to by contemporaries as the police "farce" (Bettmann, 1974), the New York City Police Department was by all accounts in a state of moral and legal disarray. For one, illegal poolroom operators were enlisting the services of officers who accepted payment for protection and oversight of enforcement. As reported in the national weeklies, policemen in the lower ranks were placed under the orders of higher-ranking officials who eventually cut out the low man and kept the payoff themselves at a sum of about $50 to $100 a week. Still, even with these changes to the New York City Police, the papers reported much doubt as to the potential of these steps to clean up the department. "Amid the divekeepers of Fourteenth Street and poolrooms of Harlem there was much doubt as to how the transfers would affect them."

Perhaps more notably, the New York police were also accused of being an arm of the Tammany Hall political machine, working with political leaders such as "Big Tim" Sullivan to influence elections. *The New York Times* speculated that the biggest shake-up in police history was primarily designed to make it difficult for politicians to carry out deals with the New York police on election day, especially since "Captains, usually supposed to be supporters of 'Big Tim' Sullivan, came out pretty badly in the shake-up." So bad was the level of corruption within the department that in time, the news weekly *Cosmopolitan* would declare the New York police "a spectacle that fully explains the disgust of those who declare municipal government in the United States to be a failure" (Flynt, 1907 [1971]).

Meanwhile, police in cities such as Atlanta, Baltimore, and Chicago did not fare much better in the pages of the press. Allegations of frame-ups, payoffs, and political connections were widespread (Fogelson, 1977), and it was not uncommon for residents in one city to read headlines detailing police scandals occurring in other cities, for such scandals only added to skepticism of local government and, no doubt, improved the sale of papers. Thus, while readers of *The New York Times* were already privy to details of their city's own scandals, the paper also featured stories of corruption elsewhere. The following accusations appeared under a headline, "Do Chicago Police Protect?":

> Gus Chapin, a steamboat man, told of a Klondike miner who was fleeced out of $1,800 by means of a shell game on a local excursion steamer, and also told of a Kansas City bank clerk who lost $600 in the same manner on the same boat. Chapin said he understood a certain Police Inspector received money from the confidence men for "protection," the amount being sometimes as high as 40 percent of the proceeds...[3]

Another headline questioned whether Philadelphia police were simply "corrupt or stupid," for either explanation could likely account for the amount of political malfeasance within the city's jurisdiction. Given the amount of police scandal featured in press headlines, it should not be surprising to learn that at the close of the nineteenth and dawn of the twentieth century, many residents of America's big cities viewed their police departments as mere window dressing that provided cover for political bosses, poolroom operators, and other purveyors of big city vice.

For much of the first hundred years of American policing, few citizens took comfort in the protection provided by local police. After all, they were frequently no better than the criminal syndicates they were hired to disband, and they were too often on the take and in cahoots with malcontents and local purveyors of vice. The prevailing strategy during these early days of policing called for close personal ties to the community and a decentralized organizational structure. Citizens were wary of the possibility of a national agency, and law enforcement was viewed as clearly the domain of local government officials. But while this strategic organization allowed for the police to become thoroughly integrated into the neighborhoods of the developing urban centers, it also afforded the possibility for too much local control. As a result, big city police departments ultimately became the tools of political machines and special interests, where police corruption and involvement in crime became unfortunate realities (Reppetto, 1978).

At the same time, and with a national heritage already suspicious of institutional power, it is hardly surprising that suspicion of corruption within early American policing would spawn a new breed of journalism that became responsible for exposing the improprieties of the politically, socially, and economically powerful. Writers like Upton Sinclair romanticized this kind of reporting for bringing government corruption and harmful business practices to the national agenda. Others, however, were less enthusiastic and even a bit skeptical. Walter Lippmann (1914 [1968]:14) described this new form of reporting as one possessing "a distinct prejudice in favor of those who make accusations," while adherents to laissez-faire politics accused this new style of journalism as "a colossal scheme to make money by doing the greatest harm to men who do not deserve it" (quoted in Weinberg and Weinberg, 1961:xx). But it was the description provided by President Theodore Roosevelt that is most often used to describe the tenor of journalism during the progressive movement. In a speech commemorating the construction of a new House of Representatives office building, the President hailed "as a benefactor" every writer who exposes political or business wrongdoing. But in criticizing this news coverage for its "hysterical sensationalism," Roosevelt compared the progressive reporter to a plagued literary character:

> In Bunyan's *Pilgrim's Progress* you may recall the description of the Man with the Muckrake, the man who could look no way but downward, with a muckrake in his hands; who was offered a celestial crown for his muckrake, but who would neither look up nor regard the crown he was offered, but continued to rake to himself the filth of the floor...

> [T]he man who never does anything else, who never speaks or writes save of his feats with the muckrake, speedily becomes, not a help to society, not an incitement to good, but one of the most potent forces of evil (quoted in Shapiro, 1968:3-4).

Henceforth known as "muckraking" journalism, this relatively new form of investigative reporting both created and reflected a growing cry for social reform. Defending workers' rights, guarding public health, and blowing the whistle on political corruption, from roughly 1902-1912 a collection of weekly news magazines built upon the thematic content of such predecessors as *Godey's Lady's Book* and *The Police Gazette* and exposed all that was wrong with industrial civilization. Exposing hypocrisy in all of its forms, the penny press and later the muckraking weeklies appealed to working class readers with an interest in bringing about a more just society. Serving as both political watchdogs and social commentators, a result of these early exposés was the redistribution of political power to the lower classes.

Yet the muckrakers were not without their faults, as one can find in the pages of these news journals articles about semi-barbaric Negroes, aggressively acquisitive Hebrews, and other such nonsense that should have been beneath any progressive publication (Swados, 1971). Still, it would be a disservice to discount the importance of this era of print altogether. The dishonesty of politicians and the bribing of public officials were among the chief themes of muckraking journalism, and these stories set the national sentiment for reform to the political establishment perhaps as much as it reflected it. And since quite a few publications highlighted the criminal activities of local law enforcement that were so widespread at the time, the printing press served as a forerunner of reform in American policing. But to understand the influence of the print media on the evolution of police administration, one must first have a broad understanding of the historical and cultural facts that allowed for stories of police corruption to thrive in the pages of the penny press, the national newspaper, and muckraking magazines.

EARLY AMERICAN POLICING (1830-1931)

For much of the nation's history, law enforcement in the United States had no overarching direction. With the public having widespread distrust of centralized government, policing was the responsibility of local jurisdictions, and the result was the creation of divergent police organizations whose shape was a reflection of local requirements. Southern states formed slave patrols charged with the task of patrolling black slaves. Other jurisdictions employed watchmen who patrolled the city for fire and crime. The sheriff and the constable were also early staples of American law enforcement that were based largely upon the English system of policing (Emsley, 1984; Walker and Katz, 2002).

Myriad social forces coincided to bring about the establishment of more formal police departments. Immigration into the United States increased the national population and led to the development of urban centers and cities outside of the scope of the watchman or constable (Lane, 1967). At the same time, the presence of foreigners threatened America's propertied and working classes (Miller, 1975). Ethnic and economic riots in Boston, New York, Philadelphia and other cities created necessities that similarly precipitated the emergence of a more formal policing system. Some scholars have concluded that the modern police department is rooted in concern over the control of "dangerous" classes, with the rapid expansion of the police force paralleling the growth of class conflict (Harring, 1986). Whether this in fact proved to be the case, tensions between the police and the public along racial and class lines would remain a persistent challenge to big-city policing.

The first modern police forces in the United States appeared in cities during the 1830s and 1840s and were largely modeled after the accomplishments of Sir Robert Peel and his London Metropolitan Police of 1829. In response to political violence and property crimes within the streets of London, Peel proved effective in creating an urban police force where officers would maintain a proactive, visible presence within the community for the purpose of preventing crime. But unlike the Metropolitan Police, whose political power and public image were reflections of national sovereignty, the American model of policing diverged from the London police in an important way. Whereas the London police derived its authority from the national government and had no political ties to local jurisdictions, the authority of the American police force derived from its closeness to local government (Miller, 1975). The American police officer "was more a man than an institution" (Miller, 1975:75). Unlike his British counterpart, whose discretionary power was more strictly regulated, the American police officer "often acted in the context of official and public toleration of unchecked discretionary power."

The fear of a police force far removed from citizen control led to the establishment of American police forces that were wholly under local control. Some cities enacted residency requirements to ensure that their police officers reflected the needs of the community, while other cities had police officers who were elected by the local political establishment. All of this was an attempt to maintain tight control over the power and authority of the nation's police forces. Ironically, the result was the creation of partisan policing that was less responsive to the public than to the wants and needs of the ruling political party. As Emsley (1984) notes, the political appointment of police personnel led to both political partisanship in the enforcement of laws and to police partisanship in the monitoring of elections. The job of police officer was often a patronage plum handed out by ward leaders; in return, police would carry out the mandates of the ruling political elite and were expected to contribute a portion of their salaries to the dominant party (Haller, 1976).

With many police jobs awarded as political handouts, the educational, health and even criminal records of police candidates were often overlooked. According to Fogelson (1977), surveys undertaken in such cities as Kansas City, Cleveland, and Los Angeles during the police reforms of the 1920s revealed that only 10% of policemen had completed high school and only 20% had scored high enough on intelligence tests to meet the reformers' demands. Moreover, many officers were physically unfit for street patrol, being as old as 70 or 80, while other officers had extensive arrest records. As Fogelson explains, the presence of otherwise unqualified officers among the ranks was a by-product of political control over law enforcement. Civil service commissioners often overlooked these candidate limitations if they would result in the disqualification of a political selection for the job.

Because a high priority was not placed upon the soundness of character of individual officers, early American policing was at best ineffective and at worst a criminal endeavor. Without minimal supervisory oversight, individual officers walking the beat had little incentive to perform their preventive duties to the fullest. Instead, they often spent time at local saloons, gambling dens, or houses of prostitution. And because these community centers were largely popular among certain sectors of the public, ward leaders often called upon the police to provide protection to these establishments while collecting protection payments levied by the political leaders. Finally, police officials were often closely connected with the criminal courts. As Haller (1976) notes, until 1906 police justices handled routine criminal cases in Chicago, a practice that all but ensured the delivery of justice along political lines.

Calls for reform would gradually change the character and oversight of American policing. After nearly a year of investigations into political control over the New York Police, the Lexow Committee published its report in January of 1895, which noted that officers were more often working for the interests of Tammany Hall than for those of the public. In Chicago, police justices were eventually replaced with a municipal court system. Nationally, the Progressive movement helped to set the stage for the formation of the National Commission on Law Observance and Enforcement and the subsequent publication of its Wickersham Commission *Report on Police* (1931 [1968]), which exerted much pressure on city leaders to bring about widespread reform to urban policing. But police reform was only a small part of a much larger Progressive movement occurring at the time (Walker and Katz, 2002), and this Progressive movement was in turn a result of what has been described as one of many "unacknowledged" revolutions (Eisenstein, 1997) brought about largely through advances in the technology of print.

THE PRINTING REVOLUTION

"The big questions in history," writes historian Robert Darnton (1996:xvii):

> ...often seem unmanageable. What causes revolutions? Why do value systems change? How does public opinion influence events? [One can] address those questions by beginning with a query of a different order, one that can be answered: What did the [people] read...?

Following his own advice, Darnton's exploration into the reading habits of pre-Revolutionary France uncovered volumes of illegal, libertine literature that played a crucial part in the emerging culture of dissent. To be sure, books had to conform to the standards set by the state to be fully legal. They required inspection by police, a monopolistic guild, and a copyright before a royal seal of approval could be affixed. Nevertheless, trade in slanderous, salacious literature was widespread. Christianity was portrayed as a jumble of contradictions, political writings contained details of the erotic exploits of the monarchy, and philosophy exposed cultural and institutional abuses. Defamation poured from the presses in pre-Revolutionary France and likely transformed what was a culture of dissent into what became a full-scale indictment of the establishment.

But by Darnton's own admission, historians can never fully be in a position to estimate the influence of the printed word in bringing about social change. For this reason, he concludes his study by asking the reader to bear in mind that, "the ideological origins of the Revolution should be understood as a process of delegitimating the Old Regime rather than as a prophecy of the new one" (p. 216). Yet even after conceding to the author's theoretical caution, the reader cannot help but come to appreciate the printing press as anything less than a truly "revolutionary medium," even if the invention of the printing press did not prove revolutionary in the short term.

To be sure, Johann Gutenberg is credited with having perfected the original design of the printing press in 1447, though even with his improvements, early printing was not a simple operation. Graff (1991) provides a detailed description of the skills and mechanisms required to produce typeface, including the manufacturing of cast type and the manual arrangement of type for print. In fact, the task was so cumbersome that it often took printers an entire day to yield a single page of text, and it is estimated to have taken Gutenberg two years to merely complete the typeset for his now famous Bible. As a result, literacy levels throughout Europe did not increase immediately but more gradually, with literacy levels in France nearly doubling between 1686 and 1790 (Graff, 1991).

In short, the advent of printing did spark important new social and political trends, but it is also important to note "how little major change took place *at first* (Graff, 1991:112; emphasis in original). Nevertheless, Francis Bacon once noted that print changed the "state of the world." Lewis Mumford (1934) identifies the press as among the key technological innovations bringing about a new phase in cultural and historical development, while Eisenstein (1997:13) laments its treatment as an exogenous variable in most mainstream historical treatments, observing that, "an evolutionary model of change is applied to a situation that seems to call for a revolutionary one."

What labels the printing press a truly revolutionary invention is that it was the first medium to create the potential for a complete redistribution of political and social power. As McLuhan (1964) notes, print made possible the spread of power through the spread of knowledge. Not only did the printing press produce an increase in literacy and education, it also brought about the standardization of information: for the first time, each citizen had access to the same worldly content, assuming s/he could afford it (Mumford, 1934). This allowed for the creation of a permanent and more universal historical record to which citizens could refer when assessing the course of government actions. Thus, the printing press is also credited with bringing about a new level of nationalism and social unity. It extended the minds and voices of the citizenry, thereby providing a model of how to add individual to individual "in massive agglomeration of power" (McLuhan, 1964:172).

As a revolutionary medium, the printing press also allowed for the dissemination of revolutionary messages. Like the pornographic pamphlets of pre-Revolutionary France that circulated gossip, farce, and political commentary, those without power would use the printing press as a political weapon to challenge the authority of the establishment, whether that establishment was religious or political. Joshua Meyrowitz (1986) has argued that the introduction of any new "mass" medium into society is always potentially subversive, as it renders the ability to control the flow of information exceedingly difficult. Thus, McLuhan (1964) suggests that print media have provided the masses with the gift of "embarrassment," where the affairs of the one become the concern of the many, and the indiscretions of the powerful become the ammunition of the weak.

The Penny Press

Although the printing press of the fifteenth century made possible the Protestant Reformation, the improvement of cartography, and the subsequent discovery of the new world, it was the steam-driven printing press that increased newspaper production and circulation. The first regularly published American newspaper did not appear until 1704, some 70 years after the arrival of the first printing press in the colonies, and it was not until the 1780s that the first dailies entered the market. But with the introduction of the steam press in 1804 came a new period of output, accessibility, and affordability as the new technology substituted steam power for human muscle (Davidson et al., 1976). What resulted was the creation of the penny press, noted for its low cost and news content geared toward the working classes.

The first successful penny press arrived on September 3, 1833. Known as the *New York Sun* because, like its namesake, the paper "shines for ALL," the paper took advantage of its low cost and clearly marketed itself as a product for the common man. Within six months of its initial printing, the *Sun's* circulation grew to about 8,000, a figure nearly twice that of its rival. By 1835, a *Sun* imitator began its own publication and by 1836, the *New York Morning Herald* boasted some 20,000 readers. The four largest cities in America each had their own penny press by 1840, while New York alone witnessed the publication of no fewer than 35 separate pennies during the 1830s. Though the era of the penny press would prove to be short-lived, its impact would leave a permanent mark upon the formula of contemporary journalism (Emery, 1962).

The penny press was truly a medium for the masses, a journalistic format that reserved a place for the lower classes on the political landscape. In his history of the press in America, Edwin Emery (1962:213) writes that, "whenever a mass of people has been neglected too long by the established organs of communication, agencies eventually have been devised to supply that want." By gearing its content toward the neglected and overlooked citizens, the "pennies" all but ensured that politicians would eventually come to appreciate the common man. The content of the pennies was often class-oriented. They noted the manipulation of government by the rich and powerful, and they eventually became champions for social reform. This, however, would require some time and some stylistic changes, for the pennies owed their initial success to sensationalism in the form of crime and scandal.

Of the pennies, the *New York Morning Herald* did much to bring about aggressive journalism to the pages of America's news publications. Founded by James Gordon Bennett, the *Herald* set the standard for sensationalism. Crime reporting became an essential ingredient to his formula of success, for in it he found stories of human transgression and suffering, a saleable commodity with which everyone could identify. When he added sex and sin to the mix of crime and other local news items and marketed these scandals as news "extras," his paper quickly became one of the most widely read in America. In time, the *Herald's* readership would come to represent a non-local and non-regional association of individuals, a more heterogeneous audience with crosscutting loyalty (Schudson, 1996).

Still, few early publications did more to undermine social hierarchies than did *The National Police Gazette*. First published in 1845 as a news weekly, the *Gazette* was little more than a documentation of the crimes of the era, but it hardly limited its coverage to the crimes of the peasantry. On the contrary, its pages condemned not only those who committed crimes against individuals and property, but also corrupt officials and those representing economic or social privilege. A rather telling example, in an 1883 issue the editor of the *Gazette* penned an open letter to its readers. Justifying its zealous pursuit of what the paper called "CROOKED CLERGYMEN," the letter provides contemporaries with a candid explanation of the editorship's overall mission:

> Clergymen have much to say about the sins of the wicked world, that is to say, those sins committed by people who are not church members. When one of their own number strays from the path of virtue, however, their mouths are closed. The *Police Gazette* has determined, solely in the interest of morality, to deal with crooked

clergymen in the same style in which it deals with other offenders (quoted in Smith and Smith, 1972:38).

By covering the crimes of the elite in the same style in which it dealt with other offenders, the *Gazette* did much to democratize American journalism, and it set a course for the Progressive movement that was soon to follow. Promising its readership that the electric light of the press keeps the morally corrupt in check, the *Gazette* was an organ and artisan of the working class culture, posing the question to its readers: "Who are the pillars of the community, and who are its scoundrels?" (Gorn, 1995). This, however, should not suggest that the *Gazette* held any true literary distinction. It was a tabloid through and through. But as Tom Wolfe notes in his foreword to an edited collection of *Gazette* reprints, the paper proved effective in presenting to its readership the underside of High Victorian Gentility, where those typically marked with dignity "are presented only as fools, hypocrites, secret drinkers, grifters, and hustlers" (Smith and Smith, 1972:10).

The penny presses of the nineteenth century would quickly make way for more respectable news coverage. As production increased, so did literacy, and education, and a more discerning audience emerged (Emery, 1962). Papers like the *Gazette* eventually vanished, while competition brought with it some mature journalistic alternatives. But the pennies did not disappear without dramatically altering the political climate. According to Emery (1962), the appearance of the penny press and the rise of the common man were closely related, and it did not take long for politicians to recognize this fact. While Emery notes that a historian of journalism is unlikely to find any political philosophy within the pages of the pennies, and while Filler (1961) argues that in terms of direct policy reform, they hardly caused a stir of any significant magnitude, they did prove effective in increasing the level of interest in government and control over its power, and they publicly called attention to the hypocrisies intricately interwoven into social hierarchies.

Muckraking Journalism

In a 1908 article appearing in *The Independent,* nearly two years after President Theodore Roosevelt decried "the man with the muckrake," writer Upton Sinclair defended muckraking journalism as "the forerunner of a revolution." The muckrakers do not love corruption, he insisted. Instead, they simply "hate it with an intensity which forbids them to think about anything else while corruption sits enthroned" (Sinclair, 1908:13-14). To be sure, the muckrakers were part of the Progressive movement in American politics. Brought about by a troublesome combination of *laissez-faire* politics and the rise of big business and industrialization, the Progressive movement sought to improve the living and working conditions of the masses. Central to the movement was the recognition of the corruption of government at the hands of business leaders. So, between the late nineteenth century and the beginning of the First World War, the muckrakers campaigned on behalf of the Progressives against corruption and greed and in favor of a more just society (Shapiro, 1968).

Muckraking journalism often falls under the rubric of any one of four traditions in American press: investigative journalism — where the press serves a watchdog function; advocacy journalism — which tries to alter the composition of public institutions; sensational journalism — where events are described in lurid detail; and yellow journalism — where events are exaggerated or are outright fabricated (Harrison and Stein, 1973). While the actual characterization often depends upon the political persuasion of those providing the definitions, the muckrakers were certainly the champions of the Progressive movement in the United States. Therefore, among the chief themes of the muckraking publications was the greed of big businessmen, the exploitation of wage-earning employees, and unsanitary food and health conditions, to name but a few. Of course, political corruption and the bribing of public officials were likewise prominent in the pages of these journals, as was police corruption.

It should be recalled that the rise of the "mass" media closely parallels the rise of the first "modern" American police forces, both making their initial appearances during the 1830s and 1840s. By the time of the emergence of the muckraking periodicals, police agencies in cities like New York and Chicago had already established close and personal ties to various political machines and those operating houses of ill repute. As the Progressive movement began to take hold of the public imagination, the police linkages to political and crime syndicates became emblematic of a social system out of control and in need of reform. Subsequently, not a few publications highlighted the malfeasance of local law enforcement that was so widespread at the time.

By the end of the nineteenth century, the reform era of journalism was beginning to take shape (Filler, 1976), and papers were already speculating that the New York police played a part in numerous bank robberies occurring near the city's financial district, including a $3 million robbery of Manhattan Savings Institution. So when the Lexow Committee published its report in January of 1895, few were surprised to learn that as the man responsible for patrolling the Wall Street area, Chief of Detectives Thomas Byrnes had somehow earned $350,000 on an annual salary of less than $10,000 (Bettmann, 1974). It was already widely speculated that in return for a share of the take, the police would often look the other way when muggers, pickpockets and bank robbers had an opportunity to make a score (Fogelson, 1977), and news journals certainly were not apt to shy away from characterizing police practices as such.

Established as an inexpensive monthly in 1893, *McClure's Magazine* was one of the first of the so-called muckraking papers to set both the tone and the themes of news coverage concerning crime and injustice in America. In a 1904 speech delivered before the Twentieth Century Club and published later that year, founder Samuel Sidney McClure discussed "The Increase of Lawlessness in the United States." Crime had been on the increase since 1881; the homicide rate was 20 times that of any European nation; and there were more lynchings than legal executions. All of this, McClure suggested, was the fault of the saloonkeeper, the franchise buyer, and the corrupt politician, who collectively "destroy the law" (Wilson, 1970:152; quoting *McClure's*, Dec. 1904).

By 1907, muckraking journalism was in full flower, and the monthly magazines were providing their readers with inside accounts of police corruption and political connections. At a cost of only one dime, the public could purchase *Cosmopolitan* and read accusations that the New York Police were accepting bribes in return for failing to enforce the city's restrictions on poolrooms. According to a 1907 story by noted muckraking reporter Josiah Flynt, the New York pool rooms paid to the police over a million dollars in protection money the year before an initial wave of reform, only to find that these very reforms would only increase graft producing capabilities (Flynt, 1907 [1971]).

That same year, *McClure's* noted in *The City of Chicago: A Study of the Great Immoralities* that "the police in Chicago...is freely and frankly for sale to the interests of dissipation." Questioning why the city was plagued by a wave of violent crime, the answer proffered was straight-forward: "because of the tremendous and elaborate organization — financial and political — for creating and attracting and protecting the criminal in Chicago." As previously noted, until 1906, police magistrates had been in charge of Chicago courts, and these magistrates were political appointees of the local ward, and the ward leaders bought and sold votes and other privileges. Therefore, in explaining the forces contributing to Chicago's crime wave, the magazine continued (Turner, 1909 [1964]:399-400):

> It was a common occurrence, in at least one court, for ward leader's assistants to telephone before the morning session the disposition he desired to have made of the various cases, which had been called to his attention. The arrangement with the police force [then] is an easy matter. The administration can be relied upon in one way or another to respect the wishes of the ward in regard to this service. And the police department furnishes a large supply of exactly the officials desired by the interests of these wards.

Though police were removed from serving as magistrates prior to the publication of this exposé, the article noted that corruption remained and would continue to exist until the ward bosses were removed, and with it the huge financial interests attracting those who administered the law (Turner, 1909 [1964]). True to its word, the next few years saw *McClure's* continuing to pursue justice by exposing connections between the nation's law enforcement agencies, crime syndicates, and political machines. In 1908, George K. Turner — author of *The City of Chicago* — next turned his attention to the New York, exposing the influence of Tammany Hall on local government. In 1909, an ex-police commissioner from New York explained to Theodore A. Bingham of *McClure's* how Tammany Hall made use of police services in an article titled "The Organized Criminals of New York."

By the end of 1913, the United States was on the brink of World War I, and the nation's presses were now occupied with international issues. Reformers and Progressives now formed new alliances with many of those they had previously opposed. At the same time, the cultural lag created by the steam press was nearing completion. The emergence of new technologies is always followed by a period of cultural adjustment

— a lag — during which times individuals must learn to adjust their practices to harness the power of the new innovation (Fischer, 1992). In time, business leaders and advertisers would work to kill off the muck-raking journals, while political leaders worked to increase postal rates for magazines. Some of the journals were simply sold, as they were, after all, business ventures.

In all, the end the nineteenth century and the early years of the twentieth began a period of Progressive reform in response to years of industrialization and hands-off government polices. During this time, the consolidation of wealth provided an opportunity for political corruption. With police agencies locally organized and under little central oversight, they quickly became an extension of the political machines and crime syndicates that were running America's largest cities. But with the steam-driven press came new circulation that for the first time truly reached a "mass" audience and worked to address its needs. Of course, not all writers at the time were passionate about the reforms for which they publicly pushed. Still, few were able to avoid being swept into the movement (Parrington, 1926 [1968]). So, for some 15 years, journals such as *Cosmopolitan* and *McLure's* as well as *Colliers* and the *Independent* pushed for political and social change. In doing so, they exposed to the public what they largely already knew: early American policing was in desperate need of reform.

Print Media in Perspective

The early American press did not create police corruption, but it did create countless "media events" in which the police were characterized as nothing less than corrupt. Political happenings become media events when various activities enter the public arena and attract widespread commentary as a result of media exposure. As the mass media are central to the process of social construction, the very selection of specific events from the vast array of daily activities represents an ideological process that necessarily places some events on the public agenda at the expense of others. This agenda-setting function of mass media means that mass media direct attention to specific political issues that may or may not result in direct action. Mass media were not the cause of police or political scandal, but police corruption as a media event was likely a precipitating factor leading toward public outcry and calls for reform.

Still, it is important to place the role of the press in bringing about police reform in perspective. In her book *Mass Media and American Politics* (1997), political scientist Doris Graber posits several "muckraking models" that attempt to objectively theorize the true influence of mass media on political and social reform. In the simple muckraking model, media coverage arouses public opinion that subsequently mobilizes policy makers to produce reform. In the "leaping impact" muckraking model, media coverage leads directly to political action with little or no public response. Under this latter model, fear of public reprisal leads to immediate action. Finally, the truncated muckraking model asserts that media characterizations spark a public outcry, but such outcry fails to produce any significant reform other than symbolic gestures on the part of political leaders.

What is notable about all three muckraking models is that after careful examination, each falls within the "minimal effects" hypothesis of media influences. The simple muckraking model rests upon the assumption that media coverage precedes public opinion, though it is quite likely that a journalistic investigation is merely a reflection of growing public concern. In this case, media are merely one of many factors contributing to reform, an intervening variable between the many causes for change and its end result. Under the leaping impact model, the absence of any real public pressure suggests that political leaders were already quite ripe for change and that media coverage merely expedited the process. Lastly, the truncated muckraking model represents an incomplete reflexive loop where media coverage proves insufficient to yield any substantive change in public performances, though it is likely that repeated media characterizations may prove more effective in the future.

Advances in printing technology during the early days of American policing proved triumphant in placing police corruption on the national agenda. While police inefficiency, lack of training, brutish manners, and criminal connections were well known prior to any newspaper report (Fogelson, 1977), the press proved effective in placing police corruption on the national agenda, thereby converting police actions (or inactions as was often the case) into media events that became a preoccupation among progressive reformers. Moreover, like the tabloids of today that do much to question dominant bourgeois values and practices (Fiske, 1995), the birth of the pennies and muckraking journals proved effective in democratizing public opinion by exposing the hypocrisy of the political establishment and providing a voice for the working classes.

No, the printing press alone did not generate police reform, but along with rising crime rates, political corruption, and a little help from motion pictures, the printing press certainly did help to stir the pot.

NOTES

1. Steinberg, S. (1961).

2. "Biggest Shake-up in Police History." *The New York Times*, October 26, 1906, page 1.

3. "Do Chicago Police Protect?" *The New York Times*, June 9, 1899, page 3.

4. POLICE AND EARLY CINEMA

That's the very essence of comedy. That's the stuff it is made of... the unseating of dignity.
Mack Sennett[1]

The idea was rather simple: create the illusion of movement through the manipulation of photography. This hardly seems revolutionary, especially when one considers that experimentation with moving images dated back some 2000 years and proved successful when using drawings. But motion pictures were different, for they promised a level of realism unparalleled by scribbled drawings. Using photographs arranged in successive stages, motion pictures relied upon real imagery to create the ultimate illusion. One part trickery, another part truth, motion pictures were the first *mass* medium to wholly blur the distinction between imagery and reality. And therein lays the revolutionary power of early cinema, for if "seeing is believing," then even the most farcical and scripted portrayals come prepackaged with the aura of "the real."

This aura of the real explains why an 1896 audience jumped to avoid an onrushing train filmed by the Lumiere brothers in *Arrival at the Station*. Unlike spoken language or the printed word, the photographs that comprise motion pictures bear a stronger resemblance to the subject matter in question. When these photographs are arranged in a proper order and are displayed at a speed of 24 frames per second (or 18, as was the pre-sound standard), the resemblance to reality becomes uncanny. When motion pictures effectively combine the printed word, photography, and sound into a single medium, they have the potential to take the penny press to the next level.

That the pennies and muckraking journals lost their progressive edge at about the time that motion pictures became nationally prominent is only partially the result of coincidence. Nevertheless, as it is a central theme of this text that new technologies are initially politically and socially revolutionary, both the medium of film and the messages carried by this new form of communication certainly did their part to stir things up domestically. Similarly to the printing press, which redistributes power among the working classes, there is an inherent power structure built into film spectatorship (Slocum, 2001). The visual gaze necessarily places one subject under the control of another. The interconnectedness of the visual image and control helps to account for the feelings of discomfort experienced by the victim of a voyeur, it sheds light on the debate over negative portrayal of minorities on television, and it explains the frustration police feel when they no longer maintain ownership over their public image. Simply put, to control one visually is to control one politically, and it is this political component of spectatorship that is the ultimate source of cinematic pleasure, for cinema allows the viewer to vicariously control the subject of the cinematic reel through his/her willing participation as a spectator. Therefore, through the manipulation and control of both thematic and visual imagery, films tap into our collective desire to control others (Mulvey, 1973).

It is no wonder, then, that "movies" — as they came to be called — became such a popular phenomenon so quickly. Making their first public appearance in 1893 in the form of Thomas Edison's kinetoscope peep show, and as a screen projection in 1896, by 1908 there were over 600 nickel theaters in greater New York alone, with gross annual receipts for New York City exceeding $6 million. By 1911, the motion picture industry grossed $102 million nationwide. But early cinema was uniquely popular among the working classes, for film effectively tapped into desire for mastery over events (Sklar, 1985). Filmmakers, in turn, quickly learned to capitalize on this working-class desire, so much so that — like the early days of steam printing press — the early days of cinema are often considered to be the era when film was most critical of American society (Jarvies, 1978).

Films like *The Ex-Convict* (1905) attributed crime to poverty, while *The Eviction* (1907) provided commentary on greedy property owners. According to Sklar's (1985) cultural history of American movies, U.S. workers enjoyed an era of unique sympathy from the film industry, as reflected in such films as D.W. Griffith's *The Iconoclast* (1910). Yet the silent films of early cinema were largely comedies, and because movies are more visual than verbal, the early film reels combined visual camera tricks with plotlines depicting bureaucratic failings so as to project a socially critical message tinged with a grotesque comic effect (Sklar, 1985). And few achieved the level of subversive comedic mastery reached by

Mack Sennett, whose Keystone Kops would prove to be pivotal in setting the reflexive cycle of police performance in motion.

KEYSTONE COMEDIES: NO LAUGHING MATTER

It is impossible to know for certain whether the police raid on the Bowery Theater Burlesque proved the catalyst for Michael Sinnott's obsession with the deflation of authority, but it certainly makes for a great story. Having struck out on numerous attempts to land a job as a legitimate singer or actor, young Michael found himself working in burlesque on the advice of a respected man of the theater who felt that the experience would finally discourage this talent-less young man. Having moved to New York from Massachusetts in 1898 to become a star, he had on numerous occasions been rebuffed by the lights of Broadway. So, in 1899, Michael accepted a role as the hind part of a horse, that is, until the theater was raided by the police and the entire cast landed in jail.

"If you do not know what a bump or grind is," wrote Sennett in his (1954:30) biography, "I cannot define them." But the fact that "the police warned the management" that "more clothing and fewer wiggles" was needed provides the reader with some insight into the goings-on at the Bowery Theater. The burlesque reduced convention, dogma, stuffed shirts, and authority to nonsense, so it was only a matter of time before the police stepped in. So one night, the police appeared with their wagon and carted everyone off to night court. Appearing before a police magistrate, young Michael had to provide a reason for his being in the theater. "I am a character actor, sir...I am now appearing at the Bowery as the hind legs of a horse." "I should imagine you'd be good at it," the judge retorted, and he sent Michael on his way with a warning to give up show business. Reflecting back on this event, Sennett (p.32) recalls that, "as far as I know, I was the only actor ever *arrested* during his first show while exercising his talent for impersonating the rear of a horse." Of course, he notes, "it was a large horse."

His experience working in the subversive genre of burlesque, coupled with his early run in with the police, likely led to Michael Sinnott's preoccupation with the mockery of the otherwise respectable. As Lahue and Brewer (1972) note in their history of Keystone Films, it was certainly in the burlesque that Michael found his calling. The respectable became the absurd, and both audiences and young Michael loved it. The encounter with the law probably did more to determine the specific target of his films than with the tone of his films in general. Still, from that point forward, Michael Sinnott (now "Mack Sennett") would share his ideas about a group of bumbling cops with whoever would listen 1972:18).

Eventually, two investors did listen, and on August 12, 1912 the Keystone Film Company was announced to the trade. Owned by the New York Motion Picture Company, Sennett was responsible for all talent, and he eventually earned total authority over scripts and the finished footage. As such, the Keystone Film Company quickly became the vehicle for Sennett to develop his passion for disrespecting the respectable, and from 1912-1917, the studio traded in exaggeration, pandemonium, and outright indignity. Of course, many of the Keystone films dealt with the pretensions of a society in general, and they did so utilizing slapstick and the burlesque as central comedic techniques. But the most popular targets for comedic ridicule were, of course, the police.

Mack Sennett certainly was not the first filmmaker to ridicule the forces of law and order. Edison's *Fun in a Chinese Laundry* (1894) featured a chase, a policeman, and a thrown prop, though not yet a pie. And a Pathé comedy from 1907 titled *The Policeman's Little Run* can today easily be mistaken for one of Sennett's Keystone classics. In this film short, a group of incompetent cops climb buildings, scale walls, and scatter through serpentine streets in a wholly futile effort to catch the culprit: a canine who had stolen a shank bone from local butcher's window. But it was Sennett who perfected the art, and not the least bit because his films featured a reappearing cast of clown-like cops.

Sennett, like other filmmakers, utilized camera trickery to create grotesque comedic effects. For one, by under-cranking the camera during filming, the final product projected movement at a surreal tempo that made officers appear downright goofy. Yet another Keystone camera trick was required when filming the (in)famous Keystone patrol car. To create the illusion of a preposterous number of officers unloading from the wagon, each man disappeared as he got out of the car and returned to the car when the camera was not rolling. When the camera once again began rolling, more officers continued to stumble out of the wagon, creating the illusion of 100 cops in a wagon designed for 10. Many of the Keystone staples combined camera trickery with real and often dangerous comedic stunts, such as showing a cop dragged down the street behind a fast moving vehicle. The footage was filmed at eight to twelve frames per second to create the appearance of speed, with every third or fourth frame removed to add to the effect. The cop behind the car, however, was real, and he had only a small platform with wheels underneath his body to protect him from the effects of the chase.

Figure 2. The Keystone Kops in Mack Sennett's *In the Clutches of the Gang* (1914). Courtesy of the Academy of Motion Picture Arts and Sciences.

All of these comedic elements proved immensely effective in holding law and order up for public ridicule, especially when combined with plotlines featuring snoozing sergeants, crashing patrol cars, and false arrests. Thus, *The Bangville Police* (1913) finds the Keystone Kops responding to a burglary call on foot after their dilapidated car explodes, only to discover that the burglars were in fact deliverymen. The following year, *In the Clutches of the Gang* (1914) hit theaters and showed the cops mistakenly arresting the mayor on kidnapping charges, only to have the crime solved without the aid of the police. Amidst all of this, however, was the greatest Keystone prank: the pie in the face. Interestingly, the idea wasn't Sennett's, but is instead attributable to actress Mabel Normand, who threw a custard pie in the face of actor Ben Turpin during a difficult shoot. While Sennett notes in his autobiography that, "worse luck for scholars, I don't remember the name of the picture in which the first custard was thrown," it was likely sometime in 1913, but it quickly became a Keystone trademark, appearing in countless subsequent shorts.

The Keystone Kops faded out of the Sennett comedy line-up by the end of 1914 and were replaced by his bathing beauties and a host of soon-to-be famous comedians, like Charlie Chaplin, Ben Turpin, Charley Chase, Roscoe "Fatty" Arbuckle, and Al St. John, the last two being former kops. Nonetheless, these films left an indelible scar on the respectability of law and order, a point that was not lost upon the Keystone's contemporaries. Richard Sylvester, who was responsible for transforming the National Chiefs of Police Union into the International Association of Chiefs of Police, complained in 1914 that:

> In moving pictures the police are sometimes made to appear ridiculous, and in view of the large number of young people, children, who attend these moving picture shows, it gives them an improper idea of the policeman (quoted in Walker, 1977:58).

At a 1914 meeting of the International Association of Chiefs of Police, officials criticized media portrayals of law enforcement, as many police chiefs faced daily public criticism from jokes, newspaper cartoons, and motion pictures such as the Keystone Kops. According to Fogelson (1977:65):

> The mass media, particularly the movies, often portrayed policemen at best as well-meaning imbeciles, incapable of carrying out the simplest order, and at worst as out and out grafters, ready to fleece everybody in sight.

But these films alone did not create police scandal, appearing as they did in an era of police inefficiency and corruption. Rather, they amplified broader social antagonisms first brought to light by penny presses and muckraking papers. The plain slapstick of the Sennett films simply reminded viewers that anyone could be the perpetrators or recipients of violent acts, including those charged with preventing such acts (Kramer, 2001). In the cycle of cultural reflexivity, then, the Keystone Kops were grossly distorted reflections of police performance, but they were nevertheless reflections.

In retrospect, it should hardly be surprising that among the first images seen by moviegoers were those of law enforcement at work. After all, silent films and the police have much in common. Films are, like police work, social constructions that are reliant upon the use of symbols to convey meaning and, perhaps most important, to convince the public that appearances are real. This is especially the case with regard to silent films, where symbolism is a premium. Like political symbols such as the flag or a congressional procession that communicate meaning without speaking, even the silent presence of a cop in film necessarily communicates the state of the State through his action or inaction. Finally, both cops and films serve a police function in that they maintain a check on social conditions. Even with light-hearted fare, films often perform the strongest of political functions when they appear to be trivial and comedic, for underneath the farcical façade lays a potent political critique.

THE GANGSTER FILM

Not every film during the pre-World War I era was light-hearted or comedic. True, Sennett's Keystone films poked fun at authority and social pretense, but other filmmakers refused to merely hint at the serious cultural issues of the period. As a colleague of Mack Sennett's during his days at the Biograph Company, D.W. Griffith listened to his ideas about the comedic ridicule of authority, but he failed to find anything funny in the subject matter. Newspaper headlines were simply filled with too many accounts of police corruption and gang violence. After a notorious New York City gambler named Herman Rosenthal was gunned down in front of a Broadway café, it would be revealed by the press that Charles Becker, a lieutenant on the New York police force, was responsible for ordering the killing after learning that Rosenthal was to reveal information about graft to authorities (Filler, 1976). Only weeks after this incident, "Big Jack" Zelig, a known gang leader with connections to Tammany Hall, was shot and killed just blocks from the Biograph studio where Griffith was working. All the while, the Five Points Gang, the Eastman Gang, the Chinese Tongs and the Unione Siciliane dominated sections of New York, and the violence committed by these groups crippled many of New York's residents. It follows that when Griffith's

Musketeers of Pig Alley (1912) was released later that year, it portrayed the urban environment as a bastion for crime and corruption.

A far cry from the slapstick of his Biograph colleague, Griffith was intent on creating a film that communicated the plight of ghetto life. His goal was to elevate the level of realism in motion pictures, even if that meant casting actual gangsters in rival roles, which Griffith was purported to have done. Filmed on location in New York's Lower East Side city streets, Griffith is believed to have modeled his fictional "pig alley" after the imposing street scene depicted in Jacob Riis's (1890) still photograph *Bandits' Roost*. The narrative of Griffith's project also captured the realism of newspaper headlines during the film's production. Because silent films were not bogged down by the sometimes lengthy process of scripting dialogue, it was relatively easy for filmmakers of the silent era to quickly incorporate current events into their story plotlines. Finally, Griffith's exploration of cinematic realism delved into the world of crime and justice by delivering a public indictment of law and order in the early twentieth century. Film historian Carlos Clemens (1997:19) describes the closing minutes of the film as follows:

> In one beautifully sustained shot, the gun battle in Pig Alley fills the frame with smoke as bodies contort and fall. The inter-titles twice refer to higher echelons of crime and corruption, and toward the ending there occurs an inspired visualization of the film's theme: a crafty, smiling policeman indicates the saloon door...a moment later, a hand appears through the half-open door and passes some bills to the cop, as the final inter-title in the picture announces, "Links in the Chain."

As a work of art, *Musketeers of Pig Alley* is truly historic, being among the first films to provide critical social commentary by blurring the boundaries distinguishing fantasy and reality (Munby, 1999). At the same time, it marked the beginning of the gangster film that would comprise an essential component of the broader crime genre. Following the release of *Musketeers of Pig Alley,* films such as *The Making of Crooks* (1914), *Outside the Law* (1921), and *Underworld* (1927) did much to valorize the life of the criminal, and as a result, they converted the street ruffian into a public hero. At the same time, they set the tone for the "golden age" of the gangster film, when citizens of the early 1930s were introduced to the likes of *Little Caesar* (1931), the *Public Enemy* (1931), and *Scarface*

(1932) at a time when the life of real-life gangster John Dillinger was surrounded with an aura of awe and wonderment (Clarens, 1997).

Figure 3. Interaction between a cop and a gangster provides critical commentary in D.W. Griffith's *Musketeers of Pig Alley* (1912). Courtesy of the Academy of Motion Picture Arts and Sciences.

Of course, one can never know for certain whether the popularity of the early gangster film stemmed simply from its graphic violence or perhaps more profoundly from its portrayal of the degradation of urban life. But the question quickly becomes irrelevant once one recognizes that in the gangster film the two are wholly inseparable, with the former providing insight into the latter, and vice-versa. The films depicted the inhumane city conditions of that period as inevitable breeding grounds for criminals. Indeed, few early gangster films are free from the imputation that criminals are the creation of society rather than rebels against it (Baxter, 1970). If one of the defining characteristics of the crime genre is the calling into question of various aspects of law, justice, and society (Hilfer, 1990), then the very portrayal of the gangster as hero suggests a failure of the great American social experiment. The gangster character provides disenfranchised moviegoers with a means to express their sense of desperation and failure in light of American optimism. "The gangster," wrote Robert Warshow in 1948, "speaks for us, expressing that part of the American psyche which rejects the qualities and demands of modern life, which rejects 'Americanism' itself" (Warshow, 1948 [1962]:30).

As rapid immigration was a defining feature of early twentieth century "Americanism," ethnicity plays an important role in the early gangster film. Upon the release of *Musketeers of Pig Alley* in 1912, roughly 75% of New York's population were first- or second-generation immigrants. By 1921, hostility toward immigrants was at a fever pitch, and the first of the U.S. Immigration Acts was passed in an effort to stem the tide of immigration as Americans began to feel uneasy about the changing composition of their national character. A tone of nostalgic familiarity, therefore, is found in many of the early gangster films, for this nostalgia represents a yearning for a sense of community that many immigrants must have felt. The attention to ethnicity in the plotlines of early gangster films also served to draw attention to the lack of any sense of national identity felt by many of the nation's newcomers. Finally, the Lower East Side of New York as a backdrop for organized crime was fitting, for crime syndicates were often the by-product of the immigrant experience (Rosow, 1978; Yaquinto, 1998).

Another cornerstone of Americanism, capitalism, also became ripe for criticism in the gangster films of the 1910s and 1920s. As the gangster is an individual who will do anything to earn a dollar, his actions are difficult to condemn without simultaneously condemning the capitalist ethic responsible for creating so much economic pressure. The gangster's illicit activity, therefore, comes to resemble a rational enterprise, and what could be a more lucrative enterprise than to trade in the very vices prohibited by the larger social system (Warshow, 1948)? Even law enforcement, certainly not immune to the desire for a quick buck, is depicted as greedy and unscrupulous. In an era of big business and robber barons, the gangster film implicitly codes capitalism as racket (Munby, 1999), with the gangster seen as similar to any other businessman under the spell of the almighty dollar.

But it is law enforcement that ultimately suffers from the critique of Americanism in the gangster film. To be sure, newspapers were already publicizing the tarnished image of American police; film solidified the stereotype. It would be bad enough for police that early motion pictures denigrated law enforcement through the portrayal of officers as clowns or crooks, but by placing the gangster in the starring role, motion pictures elevate his stature to that of a tragic hero and automatically cast him as the protagonist or at the very least, as a sympathetic villain. Even worse, if crime is in fact the product of broad-based social ills (as the gangster film suggests), then the police will always prove to be a failure even if the individual gangster is successfully apprehended, for the social conditions are ripe for the creation of another.

Ironically, there is an inherent similarity between the characterization of the gangster in early cinema and what has been referred to as the "good cop" earlier in this text. According to Baxter (1970:7), the gangster "can equally well be killer or detective, warden or prisoner. The ethics are similar, and all speak the same discursive language." Both are men in early middle age, both adhere to a strict sense of loyalty among their ranks, and both express themselves with a wit unfamiliar to the real man. Yet it was the gangster and not the lawman who stole the public imagination during the Progressive era, and it was the gangster that FBI Director J. Edgar Hoover would ultimately come to despise, until he familiarized himself with the power of media and worked to created a hero all his own.

MOVING TOWARD REFORM

In his review of the events precipitating the national movement toward police reform, or what would soon be called "professionalism," Nathan Douthit (1975:317) begins to draw academic attention to the magnitude that newspapers and other "outside" influences had on those situated within the inner circles of police administration. His article is notable for drawing attention toward early media as being among the "historical roots" that grew into the movement toward police professionalism. It was the newspapers in the spring of 1919, Douthit notes, that declared the United States in the midst of a crime wave, and it was a journalist who first declared a national "war" against crime. In fact, Douthit concludes that it was the result of "what appeared to be an increasing threat of crime," an impression publicized through newspaper headlines, that channeled police professionalism and led to the sweeping changes in the manner with which police functioned.

Other police historians similarly take steps to link the mass media to police reform, though they still focus mainly upon the impact of a single medium — the press — in bringing about police reform. Noting that "much of the impetus for professionalization had resulted from social reformers' unfavorable publicity" directed at the police, Price (1977:43) concludes that it was "the increasing capability of communications media" to bring police corruption and inefficiency to the public that "provided the necessary conditions for mobilization by the political sector." Price continues her review of the events preceding police reform by quoting Chief Tillard of Altoona, Pennsylvania from a 1919 speech delivered to the International Association of Chiefs of Police, where he reluctantly acknowledged the power of media with regard to police performance. According to the chief, "All that is needed on the part of those who would put the policeman in wrong with the public is a complaisant newspaper" (quoted in Price, 1977:46).

But it was not merely in print where police were made to look less than professional. It was the silent films of the Keystone Kops that amplified police inefficiency and characterized law enforcement as ill trained and under-educated. From 1913-1917, these films went so far as to encourage a mass audience to publicly laugh at the authority and respectability of American policing. Moreover, the emerging gangster genre portrayed crime as rampant and the police wholly incapable of (or unwilling to) bring law and order to America's urban centers. At the same time, these films elevated the status of some of the nation's most notorious and violent villains. The dawn of the twentieth century, therefore, represents a period of great significance for the history of the police, for it is a history closely entwined with the development of new forms of communication that effectively worked to keep law enforcement in check by bringing about reform to police practices.

The Chicago Crime Commission was among the first significant steps toward reform. Given the role of media in highlighting police misconduct, it should come as no surprise that it was a newspaper man — Henry Barrett Chamberlain — who served as Operating Director of the Commission, or that a former newspaper reporter — Charles C. Fitzmorris — would soon be appointed Chief of the Chicago Police. Formed in 1919, the commission had among its objectives the elimination of corruption within the police force and the establishment of a sense of morality within the ranks. Therefore, and reacting in a manner similar to New York's brass during their big shake-up, Fitzmorris quickly transferred some 700 officers. He also lobbied for an increase in the size of the police force and, although meeting some resistance, successfully added 1,000 officers to the department. Also primary among the concerns of the commission was the belief — real or perceived — that the criminal justice system was soft on crime. As a result, the commission worked to temper the discretion of the courts and corrections personnel. In time, limited discretion would also come to play a significant role in the reformation and professionalism of the police.

Within a few years, the crime wave that was said to be plaguing America gained national recognition when in 1925 President Coolidge created the National Crime Commission. Little more than a committee of respectable men achieving few accomplishments, Douthit (1975) suggests that the commission was nevertheless significant on two fronts. First, the commission brought to its 1927 National Crime Conference representatives from an array of professions working within the criminal justice field, including sociologists, statisticians, social workers, and psychiatrists. Second, the formation of a national commission to stem the growth of crime did much to legitimize the cause of law enforcement at the federal level of government, thus paving the way for FBI director J. Edgar Hoover to begin to market the idea of a strong bureau to the public at large. As will be seen, Hoover would come to play a significant role in creating the appearance of police professionalism both nationally and indirectly at the local level.

Most significant to the cause of municipal police reform was the publication of the Wickersham Commission Reports in 1931. In 1929, President Herbert Hoover formed the National Commission on Law Observance and Enforcement — named the Wickersham Commission after chairman George W. Wickersham — to conduct the first comprehensive review of criminal justice in the United States. The findings of the reports presented a strong indictment of the status of law enforcement in America's cities and would forever change the face of local law enforcement. One of the most damaging findings of the Wickersham reports was the revelation that police departments throughout the country were engaging in the use of "the third degree" tactics to elicit confessions from suspects during police interrogations.

Among the commission's 14 volumes of findings was a lengthy *Report on Police* (1931 [1968]) written under the direction of August Vollmer — an individual who would play a prominent role in bringing about police professionalism. With harsh criticism for the defenders of law and order, the report begins (p.1):

> The general failure of the police to detect and arrest criminals guilty of the many murders, spectacular bank, pay-roll, and other hold-ups, and sensational robberies with guns, frequently resulting in the death of the robbed victim, has caused the loss of public confidence in the police of our country.

> For a condition so general there must be some universal underlying causes to account for it.

What follows is a detailed specification of these universal causes. First on the list factors contributing to the failure of policing is the control that politicians have over the appointment and conduct of the top police official. Echoing countless newspaper headlines and early cinema dramatizations, the report notes how the typical police chief, while appointed by the mayor and confirmed by council, is too often under the direct control of the mayor and party politicians. "The chief knows perfectly well to whom he owes his appointment." Therefore:

> The chief, being subject to arbitrary dismissal when by any action he displeases the mayor or politicians who put him in office, must if he desires to retain office, necessarily be cautious, in the discharge of his duties, to heed the admonitions of his patrons and to follow their often brutal orders to go easy on this or that criminal or criminal gang who are in alliance with his patrons (p.2).

The result, aside from corruption at the highest levels of municipal law enforcement, was a rather short term of service endemic to the position of chief, since the mayor and party players would fire the chief when he failed to successfully fulfill his political obligations. Such rapid turnover in the position of police chief created a vacuum with regard to police leadership, providing little direction for employees among the lower ranks of a department.

A second factor contributing to the failure of policing was the high level of incompetence among police officers resulting from their appointment based not upon qualifications but upon their political connections. In language that could just as easily have been a description of Sennett's Keystone Kops, the commission called the nation's police officers "inefficient, dishonest, incompetent," and lacking any "practical experience." While commenting that as a rule, urban police officers "had nothing more than elementary schooling," the report notes, "no pains are taken" to educate, train, or discipline those who would enforce the law. What resulted was the creation of police forces across the country wholly incapable of performing their obligations to full capacity.

A third critique of early policing actually had less to do with the police *per se* and more to do with the changing environment within which the police worked. Specifically, the report noted that as urban populations increased, there was no diversification or reassessment of the duties of police officers or patrolmen. While many departments did take steps to increase the number of officers on the job, this did little to impact the burden upon individual officers. Under the prevailing system, all officers were responsible for enforcing all ordinances, creating what the Commission considered to be a near impossible mandate that would have little impact on the overall level of crime.

*   *   *

The publication of the Wickersham Commission Reports in 1931 laid bare to the public once and for all the problems of early American policing, but to some it was less a revelation than a confirmation of what the press and cinema had been publishing and satirizing for some time. Still, its impact was powerful and widespread, particularly the *Report on Lawlessness in Law Enforcement,* which exposed the third degree, physical abuse, and threats as common police practices. It was therefore a combination of factors that led to the professionalization of the urban police. Certainly, sensational newspaper headlines and slapstick cinematic satire pre-date many of the earliest of crime commissions and in fact did much to publicize the many problems plaguing early police departments. When charged with the mandate of investigating police corruption and inefficiency, it was the city newspapers that summarized commission findings. And although gangsters and vice certainly were problems facing many of the nation's cities, the novelty of cinema realism likely contributed to the climate of fear that was reported throughout the nation's daily papers.

The era of police professionalism that was soon to emerge would improve upon many of the shortcomings of early urban policing. It would also mark a period when police officials narrowed the gap of the cultural lag created with the perfection of the printing press and the introduction and popularity of the Hollywood motion picture. By the 1930s, law enforcement was improving its image both on and off screen. It is unclear whether the professionalization of the urban police force first took hold in the public imagination through the many products of popular culture, or whether actual changes in policing ushered in by J. Edgar Hoover, August Vollmer and O.W. Wilson were ultimately reflected and amplified through the popular arts. It is known, however, that the image of the professional law enforcement officer would come to dominate media and popular culture for a generation until the emergence of new media technology — live television — would once again widen the gap between the police and its public.

NOTES

1. Quoted in Lahue, K.C. and Brewer, T. (1972:ii).

5. A WAR AGAINST CRIME!
POLICING THE MEDIA

This change in public opinion in this country has been so obvious as to be apparent to the most casual....[A]udiences which once applauded when a police officer was killed now applaud when the gangster is brought to justice.
O.W. Wilson[1]

In his autobiography detailing his 30 years of experience working for J. Edgar Hoover, former Assistant Director in Charge of Domestic Intelligence William C. Sullivan (1979:83) provides a rather candid account of the strategies employed by the FBI's public relations unit to restore faith in federal government and build support for an expanded federal law enforcement agency:

> [Special Agents were] out of the office a lot, visiting the "right" people, those who molded public opinion in his territory: newspaper publishers, editors, owners and managers of radio and television stations, corporate executives, and church officials to name a few. [They] also plugged the bureau line day in and day out at police headquarters, City Hall, Masonic Lodge meetings, Jaycee luncheons, even at the local college or university.

It was, however, not just anyone who could be hired as an agent of the bureau, for the message delivered about the bureau was, to Hoover, often thought of as secondary in importance to the appearance of the individual delivering the message. "Bald-headed men, for example, were never hired as agents because Hoover thought a bald head made a bad impression." Should a man go bald during his tenure with the bureau, he would not be fired outright; he would merely be taken out of the public eye. But nothing prevented Hoover from firing individuals on the spot for aspects of their personal appearance they could control. Thus, an employee Hoover encountered in an elevator was immediately dismissed from service for wearing a red vest underneath a suit jacket, an account that gives new meaning to the expression "the fashion police."

The writing of personal letters was also one of Hoover's "favorite weapons" in his public relations "arsenal." Using Hoover's signature, Sullivan and his staff had two full-time desks operating the correspondence mill. Of course, for each letter received the bureau would first crosscheck the name of the sender with its central files before drafting a return letter. Still, as Sullivan recalls, "we were the greatest letter-writing bureau in the history of the United States." And it was not just serious letters that were answered, but letters of all sorts, concerning, for example: How does Hoover take his coffee? What kind of tie does he wear? How does he prepare his steak? The public relations unit would even draft letters containing Hoover's favorite recipes.

Nevertheless, it was not through interpersonal correspondence but through the use of mass media that Hoover truly achieved his mastery over public opinion. Indeed, it was through the mass media that he was able to repair the tarnished image of the federal government and make the case for an expanded federal bureau of investigation. Note the following strategies employed by the bureau's public relations unit under the direction of Hoover (Sullivan, 1979:84-85):

> [T]hanks to the scores of contacts made and maintained by the special agents in charge, Hoover was able to place "news" stories — invented and written in the bureau, really nothing more than press releases, puff pieces for the FBI — in newspapers all over the country...

> We also planted stories critical of some of Hoover's favorite targets...And of course, we placed stories about Hoover's congressional critics. A negative story which appears in a newspaper published in a congressman's home district hurts him more than any article in the *Washington Post*.

Moreover, Hoover courted some of the biggest names in Hollywood — including the Warner brothers — by arranging for meetings between entertainment executives and foreign leaders, simply so that he could place the motion picture industry "under his thumb" (ibid., p.88). In time, Hoover would exert such enormous influence over the motion picture industry that he could single-handedly place a kibosh upon a proposed crime fighter script. Simply put, Hoover was a master of public relations, and it was through media persuasion, manipulation, and outright coercion that he was able to restore faith in the professionalism of law enforcement and declare a national war on the plague of crime.

HOOVER'S MEDIA CAMPAIGN

When Hoover became director of the FBI in 1924, the legitimacy and integrity of federal law enforcement were in question, and its public image was less than favorable.

During the preceding Harding Administration, federal law enforcement — like the many municipal departments featured in the pages of the national papers — became a symbol for political corruption. In effect, the bureau had become an agency of presidential cronies. Agents were appointed based upon political merit instead of professional ability. Then, in 1922, Attorney General William J. Burns ordered bureau agents to burglarize the offices of politicians who were critical of the Harding Administration. News accounts at the time referred to the bureau as a "goon squad" whose special agents "were some with criminal records" (Theoharis and Cox, 1988). At the same time, newspapers were filled with stories about official corruption surrounding the Teapot Dome Scandal. Both former Attorney General Daugherty and Burns, who was serving as bureau director at the time that the alleged corruption occurred, were implicated in the scandal. Finally, both faced accusations of violating prohibition laws under the Volstead Act. The image of the bureau, as well as law enforcement in general, was in dire need of reform.

Fortunately for the bureau, Hoover's greatest achievements were not so much in the area of law enforcement as in public relations. In *Hoover's FBI: The Men and the Myth*, Turner (1970) refers to the long time bureau director as one of the public relations geniuses of his time, a man who was able to promote the myth of the agency as the supreme crime fighters even though it contributed to only about 1% of arrests and convictions obtained by American law enforcement. Powers (1983:xi) writes that under Hoover, the FBI "was venerated like no other institution in a country where even Christianity and baseball have to tolerate disbelievers." Finally, Potter (1996) observes that by the end of the government's declared war on crime (circa 1936), Hoover had converted the bureau into a symbol of national regeneration and of a powerful state resolved to serve the people.

Yet while many studies of Hoover describe with a sense of awe the "Madison Avenue style publicity campaign" waged by the bureau (Turner, 1970:113), other accounts — while still remarking on Hoover's publicity successes — are less reverent of Hoover's tactics. Sorrentino (1985) refers to Hoover's media campaign as a form of ideological warfare that bordered on the propagandistic. He notes that while Hoover was indeed effective in cultivating public support through a three-pronged approach that included the creation of media products and outreach to local law enforcement, it was the third prong, "red baiting," that allowed him to quickly discredit all critical press reports. Hoover's successes also stemmed from his *de facto* control over the depiction of crime and law enforcement in Hollywood entertainment. And Potter (1996:3), though paying homage to Hoover's accomplishments in the field of popular culture, nevertheless argues that the period of professionalization between Hoover's appointment as director in 1924 and the end of the war on crime in 1936 laid the "structural and ideological foundations for the well documented abuses" that came to be trademarks of his career.

These criticisms notwithstanding, Hoover was able to restore respectability to the term "law enforcement," even if his methods were less than even-handed. Moreover, his successes at professionalizing the image of crime fighting percolated at all levels of government and influenced media campaigns at the local level. Finally, his mastery over media and public relations during the 1930s war on crime remains an achievement that has yet to be replicated by those working within law enforcement. It is perhaps this last observation that causes so many policing historians to look back at Hoover's understanding of media with a sense of wonderment — if not envy — while hoping to pick up a few pointers.

Theoharis and Cox (1988) provide a detailed description of the successes brought about by Hoover in improving the image of the bureau and in restoring public faith in law enforcement. At the time of Hoover's appointment as director of the bureau, public opinion was largely against the existence of federal law enforcement. Conservatives felt that the federal government should not be involved in police work, and liberals felt the bureau to be a threat to civil liberties. Hoover recognized that he needed to change the public image of the bureau, and upon appointment as director, he incorporated a series of guidelines into his employee manual of instructions. First and foremost, employees were to present themselves with an air of professionalism by giving "due regard to their personal appearance and presentability." Agents were to abstain from consuming alcohol, both on and off duty. Agents were forbidden to accept any rewards or gratuities, and all were to report indiscretions by fellow agents directly to Hoover himself.

Of the changes initiated by Hoover upon his appointment as director, perhaps none achieved greater success than Hoover's ability to shape the image of law enforcement in both news and entertainment media. According to William C. Sullivan (1979:80), "the FBI's main thrust was not investigations but public relations" as Hoover made every attempt to use the media to the advantage of law enforcement. His employee manual contained a detailed protocol of the bureau's media strategy. Employees were forbidden to provide to the press any bureau information or to disclose any information obtained in his official capacity to an individual not authorized by the bureau. He issued a directive that no news story emanating from the bureau was to be released except over the director's signature. Finally, all speeches by agents were to be edited by the director. These policies ensured that Hoover alone would determine what bureau information would be released.

Hoover also engaged in the selective disclosure of information to reporters who had previously presented the bureau in a favorable light, placing them on "the list of persons to receive various releases and documents issued by the Bureau" (Theoharis and Cox, 1988). He later hired one of these reporters to serve as a bureau publicist (Powers, 1983). In later years, Hoover withheld information regarding the declining membership of the Communist Party during the era of McCarthyism because the prevailing anti-Communist fears contributed to public support for federal law enforcement (Poveda, 1982). Finally, Hoover's declaration of "Public Enemy No. 1" represented a pseudo-event timed to be released to the news media just prior to the offender's imminent apprehension, thus creating the appearance of expediency in successful law enforcement (Clarens, 1997).

At the same time that Hoover exercised tight control over the news media, he recognized the public's near obsessive fascination with crime and violence as entertainment. His goal was to "attract audiences initially through fantasy, and then retain them with scientific language and the dissemination of facts" (Potter, 1996:126). To that end, the bureau's

Crime Records Division represented one of Hoover's most effective tools in his public relations toolbox. Although it was never openly acknowledged as the public relations branch of the FBI, it was essentially that (Sorrentino, 1985).

Interestingly, Hoover began his tenure with the bureau by avoiding the public spotlight and by even refusing to seek out positive publicity when well earned. While there remains speculation as to what truly brought about his complete transformation with regard to the media, it is ironically the explanation provided in Don Whitehead's *The FBI Story* — the Hoover-supported and "official" account of the bureau — that seems most plausible. According to this account, Hoover became so enraged over the elevation of gangsters to a heroic status in the national papers, that he decided to put the bureau's own tales of danger and heroism at the center stage. To accomplish this, he relied upon the mystique of federal law enforcement and the aggressiveness of the Crime Records Division.

The Crime Records Division supplied inside information about bureau operations to the manufacturers of myriad entertainment media outlets for the purpose of promoting the accomplishments of federal law enforcement.

"True Crime" Comic Books

Years before psychiatrist Fredric Wertham began to question the effects of comic books on the attitudes and behavior of readers, J. Edgar Hoover recognized comic books as highly important influences in shaping the public's opinion about crime and justice. Therefore, in 1936, he authorized the production of a bureau comic strip featuring real cases garnered from the Crime Records Division. Aptly titled the *War on Crime*, its purpose was to convey to the public the legitimacy and efficacy of American justice by relying upon "actual case histories" from the files of the FBI. The publicity for the comic took advantage of its uniqueness:

> Daily millions of readers are following fictitious thrillers and dime novel desperadoes…Imagine, then, how this great public audience will welcome and support a strip whose characters are actual people, whose heroes are real G-Men, and whose villains are John

Dillinger, Machine-Gun Kelly, and Baby-Face Nelson (quoted in Powers, 1983:142).

The formula was simple. If the exploits of the nation's most notorious gangsters could easily captivate the public's attention, then surely the masterful work of the government men ("G-Men") could share some of the spotlight. After all, everybody loves a cat and mouse game, so why not tell the cat's story?

Unfortunately, the bureau's own comic strip proved ephemeral, lasting less than a year in publication. Hoover's comic strip creation depicted the heroism of the bureau without truly creating an identifiable hero or featuring any character mythology so necessary in popular culture (Powers, 1983). Yet his reality-based series sparked a trend in the thematic content of comic books that increasingly featured characters tackling "real" social or political issues, thereby drumming up support for varied government operations. Of course, even reality-based stories contain elements of embellishment and exaggeration, of editing and story selection. Nevertheless, they proved a powerful medium during critical times. For much of America's involvement in the Second World War, then, comic books served as a means for generating public support of the Allied cause, and stories of heroic soldiers and U.S. victories were frequently sent abroad in a strategic effort to maintain military morale. As the war came to an end, comic producers shifted their attention to domestic social issues, once again combining reality-based stories with fictional accoutrements. In the realm of comics, few topics seemed as ripe for the pages of illustrated shorts as cops, thugs, and organized crime.

From 1946-1950, comic books such as *Justice Comics* (1947), *Murder Incorporated* (1948) and *Crime Case Comics* (1950) flooded the market. Several even bore a striking resemblance to Hoover's early creation, featuring "real stories from police records" in an attempt to dramatically tell the tale of the *War Against Crime!* (1948). Ironically, by featuring real life crime stories interspersed with fictional (but not always far-fetched) creations or embellishments, these bureau-inspired knock-offs actually did more for the cause of law and order than Hoover could have ever anticipated, for they ultimately became a terrain for the hyperreal where actual law enforcement successes and their simulated counterparts inevitably merged into one (Lovell, 2002). Accordingly, in both the war against crime and the *War Against Crime!* justice was always swift — taking juries "only 20 minutes" to decide the forgone conclusion of guilt — and always final — "He'll pay his debt to society in the hot seat."[2]

Radio

"This is your F.B.I.," declares a voice assertively, followed by the trumpeting of bugles and the sounds of rolling drums. The broadcast then quickly becomes more solemn as the deep voice of the narrator (William Woodson) addresses the listener directly.

> The basic purpose in bringing you this series of official broadcasts from the files of the Federal Bureau of Investigation is to acquaint *you*, the honest citizen, with the criminal. It is imperative that you learn as much about the criminal as possible, because only one person can eliminate crime from the face of America. That person is *you*![3]

Cleverly framed as an informative, public safety radio program, there was little mistaking the American Broadcasting Company's (ABC) *This is Your FBI* radio series for a serious, government public service announcement. The program, which first aired on ABC's radio network on April 6, 1945, contained all of the elements of other dramatic crime-fighting radio programs: actors, sound effects, and of course, dramatic tales of good and evil. But by repeatedly pitching the program to viewers as part and parcel of effective law enforcement, and by calling upon the public to assist in these efforts — "Neither your FBI, nor any local law enforcement agency, can prevent those parasites from attempting to get easy money from you, the decent citizen. Only you can do that" — the program could safely proceed with its narratives of ex-cons and conmen without feeding into the glamorization of the thug's life and without the violence that typified most forms of popular culture. At least that was Hoover's intent.

It should come as no surprise that Hoover would turn to radio as a means to promote faith in the respectability and responsibility of government. President Roosevelt, through his numerous Fireside Chats, had already proven radio's ability to mobilize the citizenry in support of a government leader, especially during times of crisis or tempered faith in institutions. During the 1920s, radio became the newest form of media to dazzle audiences, and by 1926 the nation had its first network radio company — the National Broadcasting Company (NBC). Yet it was not until the end of the Second World War that Hoover felt the need to tame the medium of radio with his own brand of law and order. As Powers (1983) describes in his comprehensive review of Hoover's involvement with popular culture, the FBI had temporarily teamed up with radio producer Phillip H. Lords in 1935 with the bureau-endorsed "G-Men," but where Hoover wanted to emphasize the G-Man's adherence to evidence and bureau protocol, Lords recognized the need for action and drama, and the two soon parted ways.

By 1945, the airwaves were filled with stories of violent crooks and police car chases. Shows such as *Gangbusters* (produced by Lords) contained all of the sensational elements that Hoover eschewed while circumventing the need for an "official" bureau endorsement. When *This is Your FBI* made its debut, its goal was to restore the image of the G-Man as highly disciplined and professional, an image that reflected the tenets of law enforcement that Hoover and municipal police reformers (such as August Vollmer) were working so hard to promote. Therefore, the program, which was produced by FBI-approved writer/director Jerry Divine, featured no chases, no shootings, and no brawls. Instead, it emphasized the calm and collected nature of the government's top law enforcement officers. Despite its less than sensational flare, the program remained on the air for over eight years and presented to the public the image of the bureau that Hoover desired. But like the trend with "true crime" comics, it is likely that the many non-official G-Man radio programs that proliferated the airwaves during this period did more to promote the mystique of the FBI than could anything devised by Hoover's propaganda machine (Powers, 1983).

Motion Pictures

By the end of the 1920s and through the early 1930s, the pressure placed upon Hollywood film producers for reform was as great as that placed upon the nation's political and law enforcement officials. Whereas police were once the subject of ridicule in the Keystone films of early American cinema, the problem quickly became the glamorization of crime and, in particular, gangsters on the silver screen. Various religious groups expressed disgust over the graphic violence within gangster films. By 1933, Catholic bishops had formed a Legion of Decency, calling for a boycott of what it considered objectionable films, with the Jewish and Protestant communities supporting the cause. Also during this period, the scientific community began to take seriously the hypothesis that the mass media encouraged illegal behavior among its viewers, and in 1933, the Payne Fund issued its first report concluding that a link existed between the movies and criminal fantasies in children (Yaquinto, 1998).

In response to the outrage of various social groups, the motion picture industry's self-imposed board of censors — the Hays Office — in 1930 adopted a new code of content that it hoped would tame the action inherent in the gangster film. The code contained the following summarized stipulations: (1) Crimes against the law shall never be presented in such a way as to throw sympathy toward the offender or to inspire imitation. (2) The techniques of crime and, specifically, murder must be presented in a manner that will not inspire imitation, and brutal killings must not be presented in detail. (3) The use of firearms should be restricted to essentials. In addition, similar codes were adopted in some states. For example, half of the material censored by the Illinois code dealt with the glorification of the gangster and the display of disrespect for the law (Rosow, 1978).

Hoover too petitioned the Hays Office to ensure Hollywood's abstention from glamorizing such gangsters as John Dillinger. Apparently, the Hays Office was receptive to Hoover's requests and operated under his influence for some time. When in 1945 producer David Selznick sent the Hays Office a copy of the script for *Notorious* based upon Alfred Hitchcock's story, the office provided the following response:

> [Y]ou will have in mind...the need for taking some counsel about this story with representatives of the FBI...I think you know the industry has had a kind of "gentlemen's agreement" with Mr. J. Edgar Hoover, wherein we have practically obligated ourselves to submit to him for his consideration and approval stories which importantly involve the activities of the Federal Bureau of Investigation (quoted in Gardner, 1987).

There were, however, broader historical forces at work that likely contributed to the reformation of the lawman in popular cinema. The crash of the stock market and the subsequent Depression changed the mood of the movie-going public, who now longed for optimism as escapism, and with the repeal of prohibition, the life of the gangster was not nearly as romantic as in previous years (Clarens, 1997).

Figure 4. Actor James Cagney appears as the tough arm of the law in the FBI-friendly film *G-Men* (1935). Courtesy of the Academy of Motion Picture Arts and Sciences.

Moviegoers, however, by-and-large still had an appetite for violence and action, and the gangster genre was simply too popular for Hollywood studios to abandon outright. In 1935, Warner Brothers Studios released *G-Men*, a film that simply turned the tables on the early gangster format. They cleverly recruited long-time screen gangster James Cagney to portray a bureau agent who, ironically, was determined to shut down business on a notorious mobster. To be sure, the film still contained images of the tough guy Cagney clutching a submachine gun, engaging in street brawls and participating in what was the longest and loudest shoot-out scene in movie history. Only this time Cagney was playing the part of fictional FBI agent "Brick Davis;" therefore, the film was able to circumvent the strict guidelines set by the Hays Office.

Until the release of *G-Men*, Hoover had refused to cooperate with Hollywood studios seeking creative assistance from the bureau. The success of *G-Men*, however, provided new opportunities for the bureau to exploit the medium of film. In 1936 the bureau took part in the production of a three reel series of shorts titled *You Can't Get Away with It* that took advantage of its success in capturing the likes of John Dillinger. It also allowed the bureau to downplay the violence of *G-Men* while emphasizing its use of fingerprints, ballistics, and other aspects of evidence investigation. By the late 1930s, several studios were producing law and order reel shorts in addition to their full-length features. Eventually, shorts such as the *Crime Does Not Pay* series won the praises and endorsement of both Hoover and the Attorney General, and upon the re-release of *G-Men* in 1949 Hoover saw fit to add the official bureau seal to the opening credits.

THE NEW POLICE "PROFESSIONALISM"

August Vollmer began his career in law enforcement in 1905 in Berkeley, California — some 3,000 miles west of the bureau's headquarters. Vollmer was not sympathetic to Hoover's conservative ideology (Carte and Carte, 1975), though as the FBI evolved it came to reflect many of the elements Vollmer strived to implement at the local level: efficiency, professionalism, and high standards in personnel. In fact, Vollmer has come to be known as the principal author of the professional model of policing that came to be the dominant paradigm following the publication of the Wickersham Commission reports in 1931. This professional model highlighted the police officer as crime fighter and as a dedicated and scrupulous public servant, someone rigorously trained for the difficulties of the job and someone comfortably familiar with science and technology. In short, Vollmer's police officer was the idealized police officer.

To be sure, it is unlikely that Vollmer ever terminated an employee for a receding hairline. Nevertheless, Vollmer understood the necessity of a strong public relations campaign for the success of law enforcement. Vollmer urged his officers to study public speaking and to appear at local community groups. When facing opposition, "Vollmer had unusual skills in rallying public support and discrediting those who opposed him" (Carte and Carte, 1975:50). While chief of the Berkeley police, he was able to maintain tight control over all aspects of the department. And Vollmer was adept at building support for his many reform movements, whether a welcome change or not.

The press also figured prominently in Vollmer's attempts to reform municipal policing. As Carte and Carte (1975:51) note, "Newspapers were a major factor in reform movements." Therefore, Vollmer was probably the first American chief to provide office space within the police department to crime reporters from the local daily newspapers, a practice that continues today in departments throughout the United States and Europe. Vollmer also granted reporters unprecedented access to police files. Working cooperatively and in close proximity with members of the news media, this all but guaranteed Vollmer favorable coverage of his department. At the same time, it allowed Vollmer to plant stories in the press:

> Vollmer requested a raise in officers' salaries. He arranged to "plant" a story in the *Tribune*, with the complicity of [the editor] which implied that many "college cops" were leaving the department because of poor pay...Vollmer's program of recruiting college students as policemen had brought widespread publicity to the city. [The city manager] was angered when he read this distortion. He suspected that it was a concocted story but could not prevail against the support that Vollmer had secured in the city council, and the pay raise was granted (Carte and Carte, 1975:52).

Vollmer was quite aware of the importance of a good public image, and he worked hard to incorporate publicity into the police mandate. Professionalism was an idea in policing that not only had to be adopted within the ranks, but also marketed to the public. As such, the new aspects of police professionalism that were being tried out became instant news stories for the reporters housed within the Berkeley department, and it was only natural for them to report upon such endeavors favorably. Yet Vollmer was not in favor of creating a cult of personality but in selling the integrity of police. "He was very conscious of the value of publicity, not as personal publicity, but for the ideas and ideals he had in police work" (Carte and Carte, 1975:52). It was, therefore, in part through the popular press that Vollmer was able to overcome the very stigma of policing created in the headlines of the nation's papers. The cultural lag had wound down, and law enforcement at both the federal and local level was quickly learning to understand the media.

August Vollmer certainly had less of a direct impact on the image of law enforcement in popular culture than did J. Edgar Hoover. He did not correspond with top executives at Hollywood studios or pressure the Hays Office to tailor scripts to suit his needs. He did not have the staff or financial resources to play a part in the production of radio crime dramas, detective comic books, or major motion pictures. Vollmer also did not have the equivalent of a Crime Records Division staff working full-time to promote the achievements of law enforcement. Yet as one the nation's first truly national police leaders and as one of the primary architects of the emerging model of police professionalism, Vollmer's leadership left an indelible imprint both upon the face of policing and upon popular culture (Clarens, 1997).

Although he oversaw the publication of the Wickersham Commission's *Report on Police* in 1931, August Vollmer's career as a police reformer and innovator predated the Wickersham Commission by many years. Vollmer was intent upon professionalizing police, both in terms of style and substance. Recognizing that the use of bicycles would allow his officers to respond to events quicker, under Vollmer's leadership Berkeley became the first department to order its officers to ride bicycles while on the beat and by 1914, Vollmer had replaced two wheels with four as the automobile became standard within his department. Years before the *Report on Police* provoked outrage at the lack of adequate training endemic to police, Vollmer began a police school in 1908 that offered training in methods and procedures as well as first aid and even psychiatry. In 1918 Vollmer began recruiting college students to join the ranks of the Berkeley police department, believing that a college degree would both enhance the image and overall performance of law enforcement. Vollmer was also a known advocate of the scientific method, and during his tenure within the Berkeley department he experimented with the use of fingerprinting and lie detectors as well as the maintenance of a criminal classification system (Carte and Carte, 1975).

Vollmer's approach to policing, then, made him both pioneer and champion of what police historians today refer to as the "professional model" of policing. To be sure, an organization is said to benefit from a process of professionalization when its status as a functioning agency is enhanced, when the tools and crafts of the agency are publicized as unique, and when the social value of the agency for the broader culture is elevated (Price, 1977). As such, the period of professionalism that began with Vollmer saw the transformation of municipal police from a decentralized, loosely structured entity of ill-trained individuals into a centralized, bureaucratic organization staffed by trained and disciplined officers of the law.

Among the hallmarks of the new police professionalism was an organizational structure described by Price (1977) as one predicated upon the influential military model of hierarchical decision making that served the country well during the First World War and that expanded upon the metaphorically declared "war on crime" (Deakin, 1988). As described by Kelling and Moore (1988), this model resembles a pyramid of control, with supervision and instructions flowing down the organizational chain. However described, the new organizational structure was one that exerted tighter control over individual officers. The image that resulted from this newly emerging police model was one of discipline, obedience, and dedication, an image that was in stark contrast to that of years past. Of course, because officer discretion was severely limited under this new, hierarchically-structured model of policing, officers were dependent upon their strict adherence to the law as their source of authority and legitimacy. The primary functions of the police, therefore, became order maintenance and crime control. To perform these functions successfully required technical knowledge, specialized units, trained personnel, and police technology. The higher levels of officer education that Vollmer valued, along with his emphasis on the scientific method and new investigation enhancing technology, became prominent features of the new police paradigm.

In time, Vollmer's protégé Orlando W. Wilson would place technology at the forefront of professional policing. From his early days as chief of police in Wichita, Kansas (1928-1935), through his posts as dean of the School of Criminology at the University of California (1950-1960) and superintendent of the Chicago police (1960-1967), Wilson incorporated technology into his strategy of crime prevention (Walker and Katz, 2002). When telephones and radios became readily available, preventive auto-based patrol replaced foot patrol and rapid response became a primary barometer of police success. A strong advocate of the use of the automobile in policing, Wilson's strategy of preventive patrol rested upon the belief that the random patrolling of beats in marked police vehicles would create "a feeling of police omnipresence" that would prove an effective deterrent of crime (Kelling and Moore, 1988). Under Wilson, then, police professionalism was brought to the next level. Crime prevention and rapid response became the priorities of local law enforcement, with technology and motor vehicles put to full use in an attempt to aid in police investigations while reducing the appearance of any unnecessary force or abuse of officer discretion. Finally, Wilson was the author of a police code of ethics adopted by the IACP. He therefore strived to create a highly disciplined system of law enforcement, both in appearance and in practice, and it was this kind of professional appearance that reflexively worked its way into popular culture and the popular imagination.

The Police Procedural

In his highly influential study of the literary genre known as "the police procedural," Dove (1982:10) describes the uniqueness of Lawrence Treat's book, *V as in Victim* (1945), which Dove identifies as perhaps the first work representative of the new genre:

> The cops bore the burden of detection, but they were not "heroes," nor did they display any suggestion of awe-inspiring powers of ratiocination. For the most part they worked in teams, using the methodology normally employed by policemen in real life.

It is this very characteristic — the use of regular police detectives and ordinary police routines within a literary narrative — that Dove describes as both essential and defining characteristics of the police procedural. While literature had previously by and large been dominated by heroic private investigators caught up in plotlines "rich in circumstantial atmosphere" (p.1), Dove notes that a new genre of detective fiction began to emerge in the 1940s that was reliant upon actual police procedures to bring about a full resolution. Therefore, and unlike the rational humanism of Edgar Allan Poe's Dupin or Arthur Conan Doyle's Sherlock Holmes, which thrived at the height of modernism (Thompson, 1993), there appeared during the period of police professionalism a new sub-genre of literature that — perhaps unwittingly — paid homage to the many reformist accomplishments of Vollmer and Wilson.

To understand the significance of the police procedural to the popular image of police during the professional era, it is important to contrast these narratives with the types of detective fiction that had dominated the mystery genre for some time. After investigating the detective genre of the late nineteenth century, Thompson (1993) notes that the heroes of detective literary works were typically individuals operating outside of a formal law enforcement agency. This convention, he notes, served as a basis for the exploration of moral and social problems, much like the detectives in more recent "hard boiled" pulp fiction. To illustrate his point, Thompson quotes the opening passage from Edgar Allan Poe's 1845 *The Purloined Letter*, a story about a simple mystery that is easily solved by private detective C. Auguste Dupin but that somehow confuses the Parisian police. The passage begins with the words of the Prefect (quoted in Thompson, 1993:47):

> "The fact is, the business is *very* simple indeed, and I make no doubt that we can manage it sufficiently well ourselves; but then I thought Dupin would like to hear the details of it, because it is so excessively *odd*.

> "...Perhaps it is the very simplicity of the thing which puts you at fault," said [Dupin].

Although a brief exchange, the implications are quite clear. The prefect's assertion that the police could do well enough alone is undermined by his very act of seeking outside consultation from Dupin. That is, even the most "simple" of crimes foil conventional law enforcement. Meanwhile, an outsider relying upon his rationalism can — rather quickly — accomplish that which the experts cannot. Thompson concludes, "[Dupin's] rationalism is repeatedly valorized over the narrow empirical values of the police" (p. 45).

In contrast to detective fiction, the police procedural that emerged during the 1940s and early 1950s placed the investigative techniques of law enforcement at center stage. These stories did not, however, intentionally cast any particular character type in the role of hero. Instead, it was the techniques of investigation, the adherence to methodology and scientific protocol, that captured the public imagination. The police procedural, therefore, focused upon witness questioning and suspect interrogation, the analysis of evidence and the technologies of the crime lab, the tailing of suspects and police stakeouts. While such formulaic plotlines may underplay the heroism of law enforcement or the evil of the yet-to-be determined villain, Dove suggests that the authors of police procedurals — such as Ed McBain, Hillary Waugh, and James McClure — were able to create this form of dichotomous tension through the use of the good cop/bad cop interrogation scenes that were a staple of the police procedural.

"Just the Facts"

It is, however, within the realm of broadcast media that the police procedural is perhaps best known. Even on the opening pages of his text examining the literary genre, Dove (1982) concedes that there is no greater representation of the procedural within the public imagination than actor Jack Webb's radio and TV *Dragnet*. A police procedural if ever there was one, *Dragnet* also served as a turning point in the cycle of cultural reflexivity. No longer at the receiving end of stereotypes about policing, *Dragnet* proved an effective vehicle for those working within law enforcement to shatter old images and biases — deserved or not — about policing and replace them instead with "just the facts" culled from actual police files. The protagonist, Joe Friday, was similarly the ultimate representation (and reflection) of the new face of policing under the professional model (Kelling and Moore, 1988). In fact, Joe Friday could hardly be described as a protagonist at all. Rather, his character was merely a stand-in for the entire Los Angeles Police Department (LAPD) and a proxy for all of American policing. At least that was how law enforcement saw it.

When Jack Webb was cast as forensic chemist Lieutenant Lee Jones in the movie *He Walked by Night* (1948), LAPD Detective Sergeant Marty Wynn was hired as a technical advisor. Webb had a previous career working in radio, so Wynn had nothing to lose when he suggested that Webb create a radio program — like *He Walked by Night* — based upon real police stories. In his authorized biography (Moyer and Alvarez, 2001:56), Webb recalls Wynn complaining about the popular portrayal of law enforcement in mass culture. "It rankles every damn cop in the country when they hear those far-fetched tales about crime. Why don't you do a real story about policemen?" Several months later, and after numerous evenings of ride-alongs listening to what he described as the police radio's "unemotional reports of crime and human weakness," Webb turned to the LAPD for guidance. With Hoover-like requirements that Webb promise to: (1) never glorify or defame police officers, (2) represent police officers as average or regular human beings, and (3) follow the facts of a genuine LAPD case, the LAPD brass lent its endorsement to the project. When in 1949 NBC agreed to air *Dragnet* for radio broadcast, Webb and the LAPD embarked upon a mission to create what they collectively hoped would be an accurate reflection of professional police work.

With the opening narration informing the audience that *"Dragnet* is the story of *your* police force in action," listeners were likely taken aback by the rather mundane tone that the program took, not to mention the human, yet affect-less face immediately placed upon the central character Sergeant Joe Friday, played by Webb himself: "My identification card reads Badge #4315, Blood Type O. My name's Joe Friday and I'm a sergeant, base pay $338 a month, and I've never heard of time-and-a-half." In fact, the show was not an immediate success; it lacked the action and violence that was typical of other radio dramas of the time. Instead, and like the literary police procedural, the program emphasized the step-by-step aspects of investigation minus the over-the-top heroics and far-fetched (not to mention fictional) plotlines. The program received a promotional boost, however, when esteemed critic John Crosby reviewed *Dragnet* in the June 13th, 1949 edition of the *New York Herald Tribune,* calling the program, "an astonishing cops and robbers job simply because nothing very astonishing happens on it." At first glance, that hardly reads as a glowing review, but Crosby continues: "Quite a few crime shows now claim to be based on somebody or other's files. Few of them sound as authentic as *Dragnet."* He then sums up his review with this observation, one that speaks volumes to the change in popular imagery that now accompanied the police:

> Trouble is, most police work is so methodological it's hard to make it exciting. It's difficult to dramatize a cop searching through 400 photographs to find one likeness. The alternative is to put crime detection in human terms which *Dragnet* seems to be trying to do (Crosby, 1949).

Some two and a half years later, NBC converted its radio program into a regularly featured television series, once again starring Webb as Friday. By this time, LAPD Chief William H. Parker was a big supporter of the program, and he, along with others within the LAPD, provided Webb with technical assistance and for his efforts received credits at the end of each show. A week after the program aired on television, *Newsweek* ran a feature about *Dragnet* focusing upon the program's realism. Describing within its pages the cycle of reflexivity in which police both shape and are shaped by the mass media, the article notes that "the radio show has been such a success as an authentic account of police work that recordings have been played to police trainees in Sonoma County, California." The article praises Webb for his realistic portrayal of everyday policing, even gushing that Webb "refuses to let any of his actors except the women use makeup," since real policemen on the job do not don such cosmetics (*Newsweek*, 1952).

Dragnet aired regularly on NBC until 1959, when it was cancelled. It was revived briefly during the late 1960s until its final cancellation as a Jack Webb production in 1970. In 2003, producer Dick Wolf (*Law and Order*) brought *Dragnet* back to the television screen, calling this new version a "reconceptualization" of an old classic (quoted in Owen, 2003). But while the *Dragnet* for the new millennium shares many of the features of its early incarnation (e.g., location, character names, solemn narration), the *Houston Chronicle* notes that the Dick Wolf production, "isn't your old *Dragnet*" (Hodges, 2003). Indeed, the new Joe Friday is "not as bland," plot twists call into question the supposed smooth development of the typical police investigation from years past (Mestas, 2003), and absent from the new *Dragnet* is the strict adherence to a "limited…moral frame" that typified the police model (Fuchs, 2003).

Collectively, then, these qualitative and stylistic changes to *Dragnet* not only reflect real changes in the viewing habits of television audiences, they are also indicative of a very real movement in policing, a movement away from some of the built-in limitations of the professional model of policing from the 1930s through the 1960s. Therefore, as will be seen in the next chapter, it is no coincidence that the fictional representation of the affect-less professional police officer endured only as long as did his real-life counterpart.

In the meantime, the changes brought about by the professional model of policing to the previously tarnished police image during the political era were impressive. As Kelling and Moore (1988:8) write, the patrol car — coupled with radio technology — became "the symbol of policing" during the professional era. "It represented mobility, power, conspicuous presence, control of officers, and professional distance from citizens." It was to be a symbol that, at least for the time being, served the public well.

NOTES

1. O.W. Wilson, "Police Administration," in *Municipal Year Book*, 1936, pages 81-82. Quoted in Douthit (1975:327).

2. "The Law's Revenge! The Case of Charles Hanley." *War Against Crime!* 1:1. (Reprinted August 2000.) West Plains, MO: Gemstone.

3. "This is Your FBI – The Traveling Bride." Taken from *Old Time Radio: Detectives and Crime Fighters*, in *The Smithsonian Collection*. (Reissued 2000 by Radio Spirits.)

6. PROFESSIONALISM, PROTEST, AND PRIME TIME: TELEVISED POLICING

With TV, the viewer is the screen.
Marshall McLuhan[1]

Eugene Roberts, a reporter who covered the South for the *New York Times* during the 1960s, said that it was the civil rights movement that first made him realize the power of television. In newspaper photographs, Roberts recalled, police dogs simply looked like police dogs. On television, however, the police dogs always snarled.[2]

Wallace Westfeldt, also a print journalist, was working for the *Nashville Tennessean* at the time of television's emergence onto the political landscape. For Westfeldt, the power of television centered upon its ability to give a story an "attraction and emphasis" that the printed word simply could not. Moreover, television could accomplish this "even without any [accompanying] commentary."[3]

Jack Nelson was working for the *Los Angeles Times* and covering the South when he first came to appreciate television and, in particular, the power of the television camera to (literally) zoom-in on police misconduct. Law enforcement was supposed to provide protection to those citizens working peacefully for the achievement of civil rights. On several occasions, however, the police would clash with protestors. "What [the police] used to do, particularly [in front of] the print media, was put tape over their badges" to avoid identification and to conceal their racism and abuse of force. But as Nelson notes, "If the [television] camera got their face, it didn't make any difference whether they had tape on the badge not."[4]

Reporter Karl Fleming was working for *Newsweek* magazine during the civil rights movement. Although his news stories focused upon the same racially contentious political issues as the reporters working for television, being a print reporter Fleming was not viewed to be nearly as threatening as his broadcast counterparts. Describing the violence that would befall television news crews that attempted to cover the events of the South, he recalls how television cameramen were particularly vulnerable to southern hostility because the bulky equipment and tangle of wires rendered them somewhat immobile. "I saw these guys get beaten up so many times...It was always the cops who would beat them up...or if it wasn't them, they would stand aside and smirk while the local rednecks pounded the hell out of them."[5]

Figure 5. Still photography cannot capture the full drama of television as a 17-year-old civil rights demonstrator, defying an anti-parade ordinance, is attacked by a police dog in Birmingham, AL on May 3, 1963.
(AP/Wide World Photos/Bill Hudson)

Southerners — including southern police — viewed television reporters as threatening to their pre-existing way of life. This is because they accurately associated the burgeoning civil rights movement with the expansion of visual broadcast media. This new medium of television was different from any other pre-existing medium in that it had the capability of beaming images of racial hatred and intolerance throughout the country to individuals who perhaps naively assumed that such social practices ended during Reconstruction. Sure, the photograph proved to be a powerful visual medium, and pictures of southern lynching became an unfortunate panel within the national tapestry in the days prior to television. Photographs, however, present to the viewer a stripped down and isolated framing of an event, and they do so by relying solely upon the visual faculty. Conversely, television presents a series of events — sometimes in real time — to the viewer while engaging multiple senses simultaneously.

The emergence of television upon the southern landscape threatened to bring an end to racial segregation in a manner that would be far less bloody than any Civil War. It would also bring about a change in the manner with which some southern law enforcement conducted business. It is not surprising, then, that there was much hostility toward television news in its early years. Down South, NBC was referred to by some as the "Nigger Broadcasting Company," while those resistant to change referred to ABC and CBS as the "Afro" Broadcasting Company and "Coon" (or "Communist") Broadcasting System, respectively. It is not insignificant to note that many southern newspapers and television stations avoided coverage of local civil rights events (Donovan and Scherer, 1992). In fact, that national news crews were able to broadcast from the South and transmit their news footage across the nation only added to southern tensions, for once again southern customs and state rights had to give way to national trends.

At the same time, those within the civil rights movement were quite fond of their newfound power in television, for it was the evening television news broadcast that was able to bring the issues of racism, Jim Crow segregation, and equal rights into the living rooms of millions of American families. Reflecting upon the power of television, New York civil rights advocate Allard Lowenstein is said to have commented that it took images of police dogs in Birmingham to sell the issue of civil rights to citizens in Des Moines. So important was television to the civil rights movement that Martin Luther King's Birmingham organization would consider canceling a planned demonstration if no mob turned up to attack marchers or if no television cameras were in evidence (Donovan and Scherer, 1992:16). Not only did the civil rights movement require the visual drama inherent in televised police-citizen conflicts to mobilize the nation, it also required the legal protection that television could provide organizers in the aftermath of a conflagration.

Of course, mobs did turn up in Birmingham during the spring of 1963, as did the Birmingham police thanks in large part to Police Commissioner Eugene T. (Bull) Connor, a man whose racist views did not wane in the presence of the media. Therefore, when fire hoses and police dogs were directed toward the Birmingham marchers in May of 1963, the spectacle was visible on television screens across the nation. So great was the impact of these images that President Kennedy's subsequent civil rights legislation was dubbed "Bull Connor's bill." Attorney General Robert Kennedy later commented that those images of police dogs and fire hoses, "is what created a feeling in the United States that more was needed to be done." That is, before television, "people were not worked up about it" (quoted in Donovan and Scherer, 1992:17).

*   *   *

A Vietnam War protestor who was interviewed for an end of the millennium video retrospective made the following comments about the character of police-citizen encounters outside of the Democratic National Convention in Chicago 1968:

> The confrontation was very intense. The cops very suddenly had moved in on people and started to crack heads, and they beat people pretty badly. There was a lot of blood, there were a lot of injuries, and all of a sudden, people understood themselves as being at odds with the powers that be.[6]

It is likely that many television viewers watching these events unfold came to feel at odds with "the powers that be," especially given the nature of the televised images. News broadcasts that evening featured images of Chicago police using their nightsticks against protesters demanding peace who would "go limp" before being led away and taken into custody. Of course, sensing that the whole world would be watching, many of the protestors worked hard to provoke the police into taking aggressive action against the crowd. Activists taunted the police with cries of "pigs" and other anti-authoritarian slurs, all in an attempt to instigate a dramatic response that could be captured by television cameras. The strategy succeeded. The clash between the police and the protesters outside of the Democratic National Convention became headline news in both print and, more importantly, television media. And though public opinion was hardly in unanimous support of the cause or actions taken by the Chicago demonstrators (Witcover, 2001), it was the visuals of police repression and not those of the taunting protestors that were more prominently featured on the evening news.

Figure 6. Chicago Police attempt to disperse demonstrators outside the Democratic National Convention in Chicago on August 29, 1968. Despite taunts from the public, it was the visuals of police repression that were featured prominently in the news media. (AP/World Wide Photo)

Americans during the 1960s did not have CNN, the Fox News Channel, or around the clock coverage of the events in Vietnam, but the impact of television on media coverage of the war was profound, and it was certainly historically unparalleled. For the first time, and with an unwelcome regularity, Americans could view images of international conflagration from their homes every night at 6 o'clock. Reflecting upon the events of the twentieth century, historian Stephen Ambrose acknowledged the role of television in creating a new generation of young

Americans not as readily supportive of a national call to arms. For Ambrose, "What made the experiences of the Vietnam War generation so different from those of World War II [was that] their parents hadn't had television when they were kids. That made them different from every generation that had gone before."[7]

It was not the simple fact that television afforded Americans an opportunity to view images of war that was historically unprecedented, though this undoubtedly played a part in the creation of an unprecedented anti-war movement. Americans were certainly not unfamiliar with the horrors of war, even if Hollywood did much to glamorize war in its big screen dramatizations. What made television unique was its ability to transmit images to Americans more or less as they were happening, rather than days, weeks, or months after the fact. This newfound ability to view history as it develops provided audiences with a sense of empowerment, for if the events to unfold are not foregone conclusions then citizen mobilization holds the promise of social reform.

Television also added a new dimension to the traditional language of politics and war. Meyrowitz (1986:136) argues that in print and on radio, terms such as "enemy," "ally," "communist," and "freedom fighter" can more easily go unchallenged since readers and listeners lack the kind of visual information that conveys humanism or a sense of shared humanity. In fact, during World War II and the Korean War images in comic books and Hollywood movies were purposefully constructed to be iconic of "good" versus "evil." On television, however, our friends and enemies in Vietnam looked very much alike. As a result, discerning such events as military "successes" and "failures" became more of an ethically inappropriate exercise. This was particularly the case when the images were of burning villages and suffering Viet Cong.

Despite the uniqueness of television during wartime, it was not until the Tet offensive of 1968 that the true horror and futility of Vietnam was brought home to Americans via television. During this offensive, the North and South Vietnamese Communists launched attacks on more than 100 cities and fought outside the U.S. Embassy in Saigon. In an analysis of news coverage of Vietnam both before and during Tet, Hallin (2001) calculated that prior to the Tet offensive, American television viewers would witness on their screens approximately one civilian casualty per week. During Tet, the number of viewed casualties rose fourfold. Sometime shortly after Tet, CBS News anchor Walter Cronkite traveled to Vietnam to report directly from the scene. Such traveling by a news anchor was, at the time, quite an historic event. Returning to the United States, Cronkite once again made television history when he concluded an evening broadcast by suggesting that the war had clearly stalemated and that the U.S. should search for a way out. This commentary marked the media's first significant break from official optimism, and it prompted President Johnson's comment to his press secretary that if he had lost Walter Cronkite, he had also lost Mr. Average Citizen (Hallin, 2001). Thanks in part to television, this is exactly what happened.

TELEVISION AND SOCIAL STABILITY

As the preceding anecdotes suggest, the maturation of the television medium during the 1950s did much to awaken the conscience of America from its state of temporary somnambulism. While many Americans were basking in the military victories and political and economic "successes" of World War II, there remained many domestic concerns that went unaddressed for some time. To begin, many African Americans were indifferent or even hostile to World War II. As historian Howard Zinn (1995:440) notes, "The nation on the one hand denounced racism, and on the other hand maintained segregation in the armed forces and kept blacks in low paying jobs." Prior to the war, there was already developing within black communities an awakening of racial consciousness. Following the war, and upon the realization that fighting injustice abroad did little to change the status of African Americans at home, racial consciousness within the United States would only increase.

Many labor strikes were also put on hold during the war in an effort to support U.S. troops and the Allied cause. As the troops began to come home, the strikes increased both in scope and frequency. The first half of 1946 alone witnessed some 3 million workers on strike. During wartime, profits in some textile mills rose by 600% while wages increased by a mere 36%. This only added to the exploitation previously felt by American laborers (Zinn, 1995). Women, too, recognized how little war had changed their status within the political and economic structure. While female participation in the work force proved essential during the war, few if any efforts were made to maintain their presence within American industry after the war. "Beneath the noise of enthusiastic patriotism," then, was a growing mood of dissatisfaction and discontent with the stability of the American social system (Zinn, 1995:409).

As these domestic tensions began to fester, the power of television was growing both in terms of raw numbers and in its capacity to disseminate new images and critical messages that could potentially alter the cultural landscape. As early as 1928, the Federal Radio Commission (the predecessor of the Federal Communications Commission) reported that a few broadcast stations were experimenting with visual radio transmissions. By 1937 there were 17 such experimental broadcasts. The year 1939 saw the first presidential appearance on television (FDR opening the New York World's Fair) as well as the first televised major league baseball game. President Truman delivered the first televised address to Congress in 1950, and in 1960 John Kennedy and Richard Nixon engaged in the first televised presidential debate, an event that perhaps more than any other changed the rules of political campaigning by emphasizing the importance of presentation, physical attractiveness, and media savvy to the success of a campaign.

Television ownership increased at an equally fast pace. The first coast-to-coast television hook-up occurred in 1951. By 1955, 80% of households in urban areas had television sets. With sales of about 7 million sets per year, the figure quickly reached beyond 90%. Moreover, television was not merely growing into the nation's most popular pasttime. It was also growing into the nation's primary means of socialization. By 1959, a poll conducted by the Roper Organization revealed that half of all respondents named television as their principal source of information about worldly events. By 1963, television would surpass the print media as the primary source of news and information (Davidson et al., 1976). A new medium had emerged, and it now dominated the political and social scene.

Today, with scripted presidential press conferences, network self-censorship, instant video-editing, and even time-delayed "live" broadcasts, it is hard to recall a time when television was, at least for a brief moment, unsettling to the more traditional aspects of everyday life. Yet as the discussion of the civil rights movement above suggests, television's initial potency could be found in its ability to merge disparate public spheres into one relatively homogeneous body of viewers and create a kind of "mass" audience that previous media simply could not

(Meyrowitz, 1986). And the "masses" are always potentially threatening to an established political leadership, for within the masses can be found the precursor to the mob mentality. Daniel Bell (1961:21-22) explained the formation of the new mass society as follows: "The revolutions in...communications have brought men into closer contact with each other and bound them in new ways...[T]remors in one part of society affect all others." Television, then, reminded the rest of nation that segregation in the South was not a practice occurring in a distant land and in years past but a modern reality in its own backyard, and it reminded neighbors of their common interests that were sometimes in opposition to pre-existing practices.

It cannot be forgotten, though, that the new mass audience brought about by television was homogeneous only to the extent that television viewers now shared a common information source and a common characterization of the cultural landscape. Demographically and economically, the country was peppered with numerous cultural divides. The rise of a new mass audience would therefore prove to be a double-edged sword. On the positive side, the new medium could bring diverse people together under a common cause and strengthen the voice of the people. On the negative side, to create a mass audience and thus ensure the widest possible viewer base for advertisers, network television has to design its messages and programming to reflect the interests and lifestyles of the cultural and economic mainstream, exposing to many other viewers that which they do not have. In the end, television simultaneously ties the public together while dividing it into separate parts.

It was during the 1960s when television was most socially disruptive because it was during this decade when the new medium was transformed from being merely a radio with pictures into a portal that both exposed and reflected new and sometimes disturbing dimensions of political and social life. The transformation likely began with television's first national nightly news broadcasts, which began in 1956 with the 15 minute *Huntley-Brinkley Report*, and which expanded to 30 minutes in 1963. The significance of this event cannot be overstated, since it represents an event that would mark the beginning of a whole new era of cultural reflexivity. Almost from its inception, the evening news broadcast became a national mirror reflecting widespread social instability to the masses. Certainly, the penny press and national tabloids reported on political scandal and social embarrassment, but they did so in a manner that was quite different from the visual awe that comprised the evening news. Television also had the potential to communicate with an audience even wider in scope than the most circulated news dailies, since the visual aspect of television transcends the barriers of language and literacy.

Among the first images to communicate the changing social climate appeared late in 1963 when millions of television viewers witnessed the shooting of Lee Harvey Oswald only two days after witnessing the assassination of President John F. Kennedy, one of America's most beloved authority figures. At that moment, the box in the living room was transformed from a harmless source of entertainment into a medium that exposed the darkest realities of our own collective actions, and it did so in a way that even the most sensational newspaper headlines could not. As the noted communications scholar Raymond Williams (1977:48) explained, "[T]here are many events which come through the television camera with less processing or filtration than in any other medium." This has had, he notes, "important effects in the reporting of wars, natural disasters and famines" as well as in the reporting of politics, where political figures "are now less protected by standard communications formulas." These early years of television and, in particular, television news represent the beginning of the medium's "cultural lag," when its power to transform social arrangements and political awareness had not yet been contained.

These early years of broadcast television news also mark a time when the medium of television held out the promise to America's countless discontented that — by taking advantage of its visual power — social change might just be possible. In his aptly titled book, *Reflections on a Disruptive Decade: Essays on the Sixties*, Davidson (2000:181) writes that the invention of television sparked the growth of a "parade" industry, where citizens took advantage of the news broadcast by taking to the streets in protest. Specifically, television gave the politically disenchanted, "a prime moment of propaganda truth for their protest or advocacy when for this brief space they fill the city with their signs and portents." The communication of deeply felt injustice was born on television, for print lacked the visible drama of angry throngs. Not only that, but as Davidson asks, who would willingly choose to turn to the papers day after day to read about angry people? While Davidson is careful to note the presence of political protests throughout history, he draws attention to the uniqueness of protest in the era of television that was never present in years past. Protests of the past were "inner-directed," and they had as their goal reform. Conversely, protests of the 1960s had as their goal the destruction of barriers existent for centuries, and they expressed their demands "before the eyes of millions of American viewers." This important distinction was one that American police failed to immediately recognize.

TELEVISION, LAW, AND DISORDER

It seems that for many top police administrators, the appearance of television during the 1950s and 1960s represented little more than the emergence of a radio with pictures. This likely explains why early television police dramas so closely resembled those heard each week on the radio. With the success of such radio dramas as *Gangbusters* and the bureau-endorsed *This is Your FBI*, the police approach to dealing with television was to simply apply the formula of the radio police procedural to the small screen. The logic was that if reality-based police investigations worked well aurally, then certainly the added bonus of visuals — a shiny badge, a handsome uniform, and a black and white squad car — would add to the legitimacy of police professionalism. It is no wonder that the early years of the television police drama were hardly different from their radio counterparts. In hindsight, the naiveté with which police approached the new medium of television is mirrored in the innocence and simplicity of early police drama television plotlines.

Like past revolutions in communication technology, public officials lacked the foresight to predict the impact of new information technology on social or cultural patterns. Even *TV Guide* in its early years commented that television was merely a "timid giant" (quoted in McLuhan, 1964:309) — impressive and imposing in its appearance yet not likely or even capable of broadcasting socially transforming content. While television certainly was and continues to constitute what former FCC chairman Newton Minow termed a "vast wasteland" (Minow and Lamay, 1995:3), one can always take some exception to sweeping generalizations, and it is the argument herein that during its formative years, the sheer novelty of broadcast television news, coupled with the inability of news programmers to filter "real time" live events, proved to be a colossal disturbance of the peace.

Professionalism and Prime Time

Early images of law enforcement on television police dramas were in some respects a reflection of the image that police administrators were hoping to project. Administratively, several new features came to represent the new professional-era aspects of policing. First, police reformers and in particular former Wichita chief, Chicago reformer and university professor O.W. Wilson restructured the police organization as a centralized chain of command. Unlike the previous model of policing, where individual officers lacked significant central oversight and therefore often found themselves under the tutelage of political bosses and purveyors of vice, the new professional model of policing focused upon a more rigid or even military-like organizational structure that — perhaps inadvertently — reinforced the metaphor of Hoover's declared "war against crime" (Deakin, 1988). Second, the professional model of policing identified crime control, rather than social service, as the primary mandate of law enforcement. Third, preventive patrol, or the use of police patrol cars to preventively monitor the streets, became the dominant mode of carrying out their crime control mandate. The idea was not so much that the police could actually intercept crimes in progress, but more to create an impression of the omnipresence of a legitimate police force that would ultimately deter would-be offenders (Wilson, 1963).

Crime shows quickly became a popular television genre during the 1950s and 1960s with police officers figuring prominently as starring characters. In 1953, there were some five crime-related programs across the three television networks, comprising roughly 2.5 hours or 4% of weekly television programming. By 1961, the number of such shows more than doubled, with 13 crime-and law enforcement-related programs on the air constituting almost 20% of prime time television programming (Surette, 1998). Thematically, crime shows emphasized the early stages of the criminal justice system, such as law enforcement, criminal investigation, and arrest. They also depicted a world that was far more violent than anything reflected in actual police crime statistics. Fortunately, justice almost always emerged triumphant; programs ended with complete moral resolution as the suspect(s) whose guilt was never in question is driven away in a squad car.

Despite the popularity of the crime drama during the early days of television, as the medium evolved it became increasingly unlikely that professional representatives of conventional law enforcement would prove to be the most successful agents of law and order. Television is first and foremost a visual medium, and a visual medium requires that there be something to look at, something "happening." The subdued content of the police procedural may work well in literary circles or even on the radio, but television requires fast action, sensational images, and rapid-fire scene cuts. For police to be truly successful in prime time, what were required were car chases, shoot-outs, and sucker-punches, behaviors antithetical to the new professional model of policing. For this reason, the brainy police investigator was quickly supplanted with a brawny crime-fighting maverick, whether a rogue cop violating the precept of police professionalism or an outsider to law enforcement altogether (Surette, 1998). In time, the successes of the lone television crime fighter would overshadow those of the police as an organization, thereby undermining successes of the professional police persona.[8]

If professional policing on entertainment television proved ephemeral, it would likewise run into trouble on the streets of American cities. Police reformers of the professional era worked hard to market a new brand of policing to the American public. The reformers failed, however, to properly promote local law enforcement to meet the specific needs of the public. According to Kelling and Moore (1988:110), the approach of the professional reformers was more like selling than marketing:

> Marketing refers to the process of carefully identifying consumer needs and then developing goods and services that meet those needs. Selling refers to having a stock of products or goods on hand irrespective of need and selling them. The reform strategy had as its starting point a set of police tactics (services) that police promulgated...for the purpose of establishing internal control.

By the 1960s, the new policing strategies contributed to the already growing social conflict within the nation's urban communities. While officer discretion was to be replaced with a strict adherence to the law under the new model of policing, many citizens felt that the police had different arrest policies according to race (Bayley and Mendehlson, 1971). Findings from the Kerner Commission, an investigative body formed in 1967 to study and improve race relations within the United States, only added support to these claims, indicating that at all ages, blacks were far more critical of the police than whites. Specifically, black citizens were more likely to believe that the police used insulting language, that they stopped and frisked individuals for no apparent reason, and that they roughed people up unnecessarily (National Advisory Commission on Civil Disorders, 1968). During the 1960s, the language used to describe relations between the police and the citizenry was increasingly couched in metaphors of war. Black residents living in the urban ghettos viewed the police as an army of occupation, a perception that was hard for police to shake given their adherence to preventive patrol — a strategy that required police to periodically monitor the streets while patrolling in their tank-like squad cars. Moreover, the emphasis on both the patrol car and police technology in general created a physical barrier between law enforcement officers and the communities they served, rendering the police impersonal and soldier-like (Walker and Katz, 2000). Finally, political protesters came to view the police as tools of the powerful members of society since it was the job of the police to maintain order (i.e., "the status quo"). What often resulted, however, was simply the silencing of dissent (Cooper et al., 1975).

The rise of domestic civil unrest and the failure of police professionalism to cope with the demands of the visual medium of television combined to seriously undermine the image of the police as the embodiment of a civil society that dominated the early years of the crime drama. A by-product of police professionalism was that inner city residents came to view the police as an occupying force, and police attitudes toward the public only confirmed the "us versus them" mentality. Studies of police perceptions of the public conducted during the 1960s revealed widespread police cynicism toward the overall character of the community residents (Skolnick, 1974). Tensions within African-American communities toward the white establishment began to rise prior to and during the Second World War, and they reached a tipping point in the years following the war's completion when attention was directed inward. Finally, television had yet to become crystallized as a tool solely within the grasp of political pundits and press secretaries whose pre-planned media events determined the scope of the reporting on current events. For a brief moment in its history, then, television would prove to be less a timid giant than a medium whose power that threatened to topple reigning giants.

Broadcasting Unrest

The civil rights protests in the South, the assassination of a U.S. president, and the politics of the Vietnam War represent only a fraction of the real-life drama to be broadcast on network television during the formative years of television. If those years had been more peaceful, the evolution of policing might have taken somewhat of a different turn. Or maybe the transformation from professional to "community" style policing would simply have been delayed for some years, only to emerge at some other moment in time out of necessity and inevitability. Whatever the case might have been, the 1960s did experience a series of urban riots in such cities as Los Angeles, Detroit, and Newark, and these events contained the visuals necessary for the new medium of television. Unfortunately for police, footage of urban unrest juxtaposed with images of officers in riot gear only reinforced the sense that law enforcement represented an occupying army within America's inner cities.

In August of 1965, Watts, an area in the South Central part of Los Angeles, experienced six days of rioting that resulted in almost 4,000 arrests, 1,000 injuries, and 34 deaths. Virtually all participants were black. By the end of the rioting, police and the National Guard sealed off an area covering over 46 square miles. Some 934 police, 719 sheriff deputies, and 13,900 National Guard troops were called to restore order. The rioting was touched off when police pulled over Marquette Frye for reckless driving. When police ascertained that Frye had been under the influence of alcohol and moved to make an arrest, Frye became belligerent, leading one of the officers to use his baton against Frye. As the summer heat typically drew individuals outside of their apartments and houses and onto the streets, many local residents witnessed Frye's arrest. When a backup officer arrived and assisted in delivering blows to a recalcitrant Frye, the eyewitnesses to the arrest became increasingly angry. One of the officers felt someone spit upon him, and he pulled from the crowd the person he suspected was responsible — a young woman in a barber's smock that was likely mistaken by the crowd as a maternity dress. It was this action that sparked the throwing of rocks, bottles, and bricks by the crowd, and the rioting quickly began. During the next six days, the Watts Riots were covered extensively on television, and many commentators later blamed sensational television coverage for inciting viewers to join those already engaging in acts of civil unrest (Sears and McConahay, 1973).

The Detroit riots similarly lasted about six days and occurred in a mostly black neighborhood. According to the *Report* of the National Advisory Commission on Civil Disorders (1968), in July 1967 the Detroit police raided a private social club that had a reputation for after hours drinking and gambling. They expected to find only a couple dozen patrons, but a celebration for a returned Vietnam serviceman was underway, and police were faced with the task of making some 80 arrests. It was more than an hour before all patrons could be transported to the police station; during this time, a crowd of about 200 community members gathered outside the club. While nothing else of significance occurred that night between the police and the community to trigger rioting, the location of the social club targeted by police had special significance for many area black residents. A month earlier, the killing of a black prostitute in that area was determined by police to have been committed by a pimp. Community members, however, believed that the prostitute had actually been killed by a vice officer. Similarly, in the month prior to the police raid, a black man had been killed by a group of white youths. While the police did arrest a suspect, many blacks in the community questioned why the police did not arrest all of the youths. The perception was that police were providing differential and substandard treatment because the victim was black. The family of the slain man lived only blocks from 12th Street.

Upon the arrest of the final club patron, a member of the gathering crowd shouted, "We're going to have a riot!" Less than an hour later, the size of the crowd was in the thousands as many began window smashing and looting. By this time, police presence in or around the riot area grew to 369 officers. As the rioting escalated, the National Guard was brought into Detroit and Governor Romney declared a state of public emergency. At the height of the violence, President Johnson authorized the deployment of paratroopers into the city. By the end of the rioting six days later, damage to both persons and property was extensive. According to the *Report* of the National Advisory Commission on Civil Disorders, 43 deaths were attributed to the riots, all but 10 of whom were black, and police actions accounted for at least 20 of the fatalities, while one officer fell victim to "friendly fire." Churches, businesses, and private dwellings suffered extensive damage or destruction, with estimates of rebuilding costs in the tens of millions of dollars (National Advisory Commission on Civil Disorders, 1968).

Figure 7. Did television coverage of rioting undermine the authority of the police? Demonstrators push against a police car after rioting erupted in a crowd of 1,500 in the Los Angeles area of Watts, August 12, 1965. (AP/World Wide Photo)

Unfortunately, and despite the widespread damage caused by the Watts and Detroit riots, rioting during the 1960s was not limited to these two isolated events. The year 1966 alone witnessed 11 major riots (i.e., riots lasting two days or longer) and 32 minor riots. In 1967, there were 25 major riots and 30 minor riots. Clearly, something was causing rioting to spread. In response to criticisms that television played a part in the spread of disorder in Watts, some Detroit broadcasters initially decided not to report the riot during its early development. Of course, it would be foolish to presuppose that but for the existence of television, conditions would not be in place for the transformation of relatively routine arrests into widespread social conflict. As noted in the report of the National Advisory Commission on Civil Disorders (1968) — also known as the Kerner Commission — like other cities experiencing rioting during the 1960s, Detroit was in the midst of rapid social and economic transformation at the time the rioting erupted. Middle-class whites were leaving the city and moving to the suburbs; in the seven years prior to the rioting, the black population in Detroit rose by 10%, schools became overcrowded, and there was a shortage of skilled workers and economic resources. The role of television, then, must be assessed not in terms of whether it sparked the riots of the 1960s — it clearly did not — but whether it contributed to their duration, their expansion, and the sense that the police were ill equipped or simply unwilling to act "professionally" in response to these outbreaks.

There is no shortage of theorizing as to the impact of television on the occurrence of social unrest during the 1960s. Comparing riots or protests "with or without live or extensive [television] coverage is not likely to yield a reliable answer to the question" (Lang and Lang, 1972:99). This has not prevented urban historians and media scholars from attempting to ascertain mass media's contribution — if any — to the occurrence or spread of civil unrest. In their investigation into the relationship between collective violence and the news media, Lang and Lang (1972) begin their discussion conservatively by correctly noting that television did not create the underlying conditions leading to racial tension and minority groups' distrust of authority, and it certainly did not invent the practice of taking to the streets. Nevertheless, they argue that television did provide otherwise disenfranchised citizens with a "useful substitute" for conventional lobbying. Stated differently, "Officials who ignore a petition with thousands of signatures sometimes find it difficult not to react to a far smaller demonstration that enjoys the spotlight of media publicity" (p.97). They conclude that, at a minimum, the mass media and television in particular promote the awareness of protest and social unrest that often occurs outside of the viewer's own community and draw attention to political events that may otherwise go unnoticed. At its best, television serves as a powerful ally for the socially disenfranchised by providing a mechanism through which individuals can score points against opposition by "embarrassing recalcitrant authorities."

More extreme arguments regarding the role of television in social protests and urban riots posit that broadcast news incites collective violence. The report of the National Commission on the Causes and Prevention of Violence (1969) argued that "There is little doubt" that television coverage "has an effect on the behavior of protestors." The belief is that demonstrators and rioters will perform in the front of the camera to play to a television audience, and to some degree, this is certainly true. As previously mentioned, protestors outside the Democratic National Convention in Chicago worked hard to incite police violence in front of the television cameras. But Feagin and Harlan (1973:169) cite research included in the *Report* of the National Advisory Commission on Civil Disorders suggesting that — despite popularly held beliefs — television news did not sensationalize the urban riots. Instead, television coverage focused primarily upon the activities of law enforcement officers acting in their capacity as agents of social control. "[B]lack militants did not constitute the majority of news interviews." Rather, news coverage of rioting featured "frequent interviews with white police officials and other public authorities" (Feagin and Harlan, 1973:169). Ironically, the commission failed to consider that the exclusion of "militant" blacks by the media in favor of white police officers may have actually contributed to racial hostility during the rioting because of the media's failure to air the concerns of inner-city residents.

Perhaps the most widely held perspective regarding the role of media on social unrest is that television represents one of its many "accelerating causes" (Banfield, 1970). Stated differently, there was nothing about television *per se* that sparked social outburst in urban areas such as Watts, Newark, or Detroit (though Chicago may be an exception). Rather, a long history of social conditions, coupled with pent-up frustrations — or as Banfield (1970) argues, sheer opportunism — contributed to the initial conflagration. Television, then, only served as a mechanism contributing to the social contagion of riots and demonstration, though the importance of even this qualified role of television cannot be diminished, for images of lawlessness disseminated to a national audience had a profound effect on public assessments of police professionalism. The mayor of Plainfield, New Jersey noted following the Newark riots, "The sensational coverage of the Newark riot showed persons looting stores while the police took no action to halt them" (quoted in Banfield, 1970:198). Banfield (1970:199) argues that because television beamed images of widespread lawlessness, "The rioters knew that they had little or nothing to fear from the police." Moreover:

> Under pressure from the civil rights movement...and as the result of the growing "professionalism" of police administrators... the patrolman's discretion in the use of force declined...During a riot, the police were especially ineffective...Sometimes the police had to stand by and allow looting to go on before their eyes. This, of course, increased the tempo of the rioting.

Television, then, becomes the vehicle that carries messages of social unrest to a wider audience, thus paving the way for an ever-expanding movement. Because rioters and demonstrators typically comprise previously disenfranchised groups and voices not commonly featured in the media, television alone, simply by covering an event, can become a more effective spokesperson than any individual "militant" interviewed on the medium. When images of social unrest are juxtaposed with footage of police either standing on the sidelines or employing what appears to be excessive force, the legitimacy and professionalism of the police are bound to diminish.

The police were previously symbols of order and control, but the public was now exposed to unrehearsed performances of police professionalism that resembled the antithesis of control. Images of police officers using their batons against the public "did not make good press to say the least" (Geller et al., 1994:7). The National Commission on the Causes and Prevention of Violence (1969) argued that the presence of media during civil disorder may have caused police to "play to the television audience," thereby exacerbating public tensions and the appearance of official impropriety. The report went on to note that prior to the disorders in Watts, Detroit and Newark, "police were trained to act as individual groups of two and three. This training was clearly inadequate to deal with the massive disturbance which required a well disciplined force acting in unison" (p. 104). Yet it was these very disturbances that were featured on television and that threatened the legitimacy of police professionalism by bringing images of ill-trained officers into the living rooms of so many Americans.

To be sure, the media were aware of hundreds of protests and social disturbances during the 1960s that did not involve violent encounters between the police and the public. The visual bias of the new television format, however, meant that news editors would not dispatch camera crews unless violence was already in progress (Epstein, 1974). Therefore, the ability of television to expose unrehearsed images of police performances proved once again to undermine the legitimacy of law enforcement, and police professionalism specifically. It quickly became clear that any successful strategy of contemporary policing required a near complete command of the police image much in the way that Hoover had exercised control over the image of the FBI in film, in print, and on the radio during his tenure. Police input into the newsmaking process was to become a starting point and an area of central importance during the transition between the professional and developing community-policing eras (Ziembo-Vogl, 1998).

NOTES

1. McLuhan, M. (1964).

2. Donovan, R.J. and R. Scherer (1992).

3. Quoted in Donovan, R.J. and R. Scherer (1992:6).

4. Quoted in Donovan, R.J. and R. Scherer (1992:6).

5. Quoted in Donovan, R.J. and R. Scherer (1992:12).

6. ABC News/History Channel (1999). *The Century: America's Time.* (Video recording.) New York: ABC Video.

7. ibid.

8. It is interesting to note that during the 2002-2003 television season, among the top primetime programs were the criminal justice-themed *CSI: Crime Scene Investigation* and *Law and Order.* While neither the *CSI* nor *Law and Order* franchises feature the violent car chases and shoot-outs of more traditional cop shows and often resemble the police procedural, neither franchise constitutes the *cop genre* in the traditional sense. The former program focuses upon the skills of those working within a county forensics lab, while the latter focuses upon detectives (not street cops) and concentrates heavily upon courtroom drama.

7. FROM POLICE OFFICER TO SPIN DOCTOR: CONTEMPORARY POLICE-MEDIA RELATIONS[1]

> *There is no intrinsic reason... why the constructions of*
> *reality by public relations specialists should be thought of*
> *as any different from those in any group in the business of*
> *telling stories.*
> Robert Jackall[2]

Describing themselves as "one of the leading law enforcement agencies in the country," the "Urbandale" Police Department is also a national leader in terms of its ability to shape the content of media to meet its organizational needs. Serving a city of a half million residents, the department functions in one of the nation's largest media markets, where an understanding of how the news media operate is truly essential. Therefore, Urbandale Police have incorporated into their administrative framework a comprehensive media-relations office staffed with six employees (three full-time sworn officers and three civilian support staff) whose sole responsibilities are to cooperate with reporters and utilize the media to their fullest advantage. And these employees are certainly put to good use. On average, the staff fields daily media inquiries from 27 different reporters representing as many as 24 different media outlets. Moreover, because news is a 24/7 operation, the Urbandale media-relations staff is on call around the clock to respond to "breaking events" whenever they should occur.

To prepare for the demands of this concentrated media market, Urbandale media spokespersons, or police public information officers (PIOs) as they are commonly called, receive approximately 40 hours of formal media training each year through external coursework offered by private consulting firms or directly through the International Association of Chiefs of Police (IACP), which now has a special division of PIOs. During training, PIOs learn the basics of the newsmaking process, including how wire services function, the differences between local and large metropolitan newspapers, and the challenges of various media formats. Training manuals and coursework devote much time to educating officers about the requirements of broadcast news. For instance, one manual distributed to Urbandale PIOs during their media training coursework reads as follows:

> Because TV reporters are by far the most demanding and the most irritating, this manual and...media relations [course focuses] largely on helping you with the television medium. Fact is, if you can handle TV reporters you can handle 'em all. But there are other reporters with whom you will come into contact and you need to know a little about their types of media, too.

PIOs also learn to rehearse sound bites and to "parade" apprehended suspects in front of the cameras for positive news play:

> With practice, a skilled chief or PIO can partially control media coverage by delivering one or two such sound bites in a prepared statement. Reporters hear those nuggets go by, write them down or make mental notes that they're there, and will often use those spoon-fed sound bites; make it easy for them, and you can sometimes exercise another measure of control over them.

> [P]arading defendants for the TV cameras [is a] harmless [act] of cooperation with the media which show[s] law enforcement in a positive light (doing its job) while *not* jeopardizing an individual defendant's right to a fair trial or his right to privacy.

Most importantly, PIOs learn how to plan ahead for "the ugly," a euphemism for the inevitable police scandal:

> [I]n an ugly situation, your natural inclination may be to lock out the media and the public, but you must *never* do that...[I]f you hide, stonewall, play armadillo, the media will perceive and report this as a clear admission of terrible wrongdoing and guilt, and you will be convicted in the court of public opinion in half a heartbeat. Your relationship with the media and the public will be in a hole so deep you'll have to stand on a chair just to reach bottom...So the first critical thing to remember in handling an ugly situation is, **DON'T HIDE IT!**...In fact, in some cases, as soon as trouble hits, you can actually turn what *looks* like an ugly situa-

tion into a positive that works to your advantage, by going proactive.

Because officers receive formal media training only one week per year, the Urbandale media-relations office maintains its own news library where PIOs can routinely engage in reflexive policing. Included in the library are department-related newspaper clippings as well as videotapes of local news broadcasts that are recorded by the 13 televisions and video recorders set up within their office conference room. As part of their daily function, the PIOs review the new additions to their library while critiquing the quality of their performances by monitoring both the sound bites given and the image(s) projected by their on-screen presence. Their assessments, however, are not limited to their own performances. Urbandale PIOs also review videotapes of national law enforcement news stories featured on CNN, MSNBC, and other cable news networks, as national coverage of law enforcement more typically focuses upon "the ugly." The goal in monitoring both local and national news is to uncover and incorporate what "works" in maintaining a positive police image from the myriad media images reflected back to them on their array of in-office television screens, while avoiding that which deflects from their department's organizational needs.

In terms of a comprehensive media strategy, Urbandale's approach to communicating with members of the news media is two-fold. On one front, Urbandale PIOs serve as spokespersons for the department by simply providing reporters with information about local crimes and other law enforcement-related activities, all the while working hard to frame their sound bites in a perspective that is intended to promote the department. But to avoid the impression that they are merely "talking heads," Urbandale PIOs do not handle media interviews exclusively; instead, they may defer to the crime scene commander or to the responding officer while merely providing technical assistance by suggesting possible news frames. Regardless of who within the department actually delivers the sound bite, the goal is ensure that the information delivered to the public originates from the police and not from a second or third party — such as an eyewitness or a defense attorney — who may be critical of police practices.

On a second front, the Urbandale media-relations office engages in proactive media contacts and notably creative public relations to sell the image of the department to the public. On one occasion, an Urbandale PIO made a "mystery guest deejay" appearance on a local morning radio show. Listeners were given an opportunity to call into the station and play "20-questions" with the guest in an attempt to ascertain the celebrity identity. In return, the winner received two front-row concert tickets with limousine service to the event. Due to the high visibility of Urbandale PIOs, it only took minutes before a caller identified the mystery guest as none other than "Daryl," a young and witty Urbandale PIO who had risen to the level of celebrity status within the community. Indeed, his high visibility allowed him to be voted "one of television's sexiest men" by a local morning news show.

POLICE AND THE NEWSMAKING PROCESS

It would be an overstatement to suggest that all or even most police departments display the kind of media savvy or *proactive* (i.e., pre-media scandal) reflexive policing evidenced in the above anecdote about the Urbandale Police Department. As the history of police-media relations (and hopefully, this book) suggests, although police regularly engage in cultural reflexivity, they have traditionally adopted a reactive approach toward using the media for purposes of public relations. While they have on occasion cooperated with Hollywood to produce such television programs as *Dragnet* or to provide technical assistance on films to enhance their public image, they have engaged in impression management only when confronted with scandal. As a result, police public relations has — until recently — been primarily for the purposes of damage control, while everyday police interaction with news reporters has been limited to publicizing neighborhood crime or requesting community assistance in crime prevention.

Several factors can account for police reticence with regard to proactively confronting the news media, especially for the purpose of public relations. At the most basic level, there has been a profound failure on the part of police to understand the centrality of media in a free society, not to mention the importance of media to the maintenance of the legitimacy of public officials — including the police. Too often, police maintain the position that reporters constitute the enemy and approach the requirement of police-media interaction with an air of resentment. They may even work hard to find ways to avoid contact with reporters by limiting the amount of information they release about important events, only to express puzzlement when further inquiries come in. For example, one PIO from "Morganville," a city of one million residents with a police force embroiled in scandal, described his approach to dealing with reporters this way:

> I will release enough information to media to meet their immediate needs, and I say to myself, "That'll hold 'em 'til tomorrow." But when they call back the next day and ask if there is any new information and I tell them "no," they get mad.

At the same time, and with much justification, police may avoid news reporters because of a belief that the news media have a misunderstanding of the role of law enforcement in society. That is, media are prone to portray law enforcement exclusively as crime fighters while simultaneously sensationalizing violent criminal incidents in headlines, a juxtaposition that can undermine the appearance of police effectiveness in maintaining public safety. Daryl, the Urbandale PIO, expressed concern that the public perceives the officers he represents solely as officers instead of as individuals who are both human and fallible.

> One of the important things that's been very important...is to try and move away from simply being a police officer; it's in our television persona, it's in what we do in the radio, and it's in what we do in the community. We try to go away from just a police officer's persona. We try to let people know that...outside of the uniform we're John Q. Citizen, we're just like the people we're trying to reach. But by the same token, we're highly trained law enforcement officers.

Finally, there remains a belief among many officers that working with the news media falls outside of the scope of traditional everyday police work. Again, this view was made explicit by those working within the Morganville Police Department, as expressed by the lieutenant in charge of media relations:

> Sometimes I get confused who I work for. But I try to let my officers know that I work for them, not the media. And the media should make no mistake about the fact that I work for the police department first and foremost. I am an officer...It's neat when

friends say, "Hey, I saw you on TV," but I don't give a shit about that. I'm a cop. A street cop.

For all of these reasons, police have been known to deal with news reporters at a distance while withholding certain facts, cutting off access to particular reporters or establishing a level of organizational secrecy. Ericson et al. (1989) summarize this sometimes tense police-media relationship as constituting a negotiation over the control of news content and, by extension, a negotiation over the quality of the police image.

It is ironic, then, that despite the high level of suspicion that traditionally accompanied their interaction with news reporters, police tend to benefit from news media coverage of law enforcement practices. To understand this requires a cursory understanding of the newsmaking process. News organizations call upon journalists to provide accounts of community events on a routine basis. This requires a high level of dependence upon and cooperation with government officials, including the police, who comprise the bulk of news sources and who provide the necessary news accounts (Gans, 1979). To ensure a constant supply of news items and authoritative sources, journalists maintain an "index of voices" and viewpoints for both news and editorials that may be readily accessed at any given point in the newsmaking process. This journalistic dependence upon public officials works to the benefit of government agencies by routinely affording them privileged status in the marketplace of ideas, allowing them to frame news events according to their organizational needs (Bennett, 1990).

Police are routinely key participants in the newsmaking process and, despite some reservations, they represent the primary sources for the production of crime news (Sherizen, 1978; Fishman, 1980; Chibnall, 1981; Barak, 1988; Ericson et al., 1989; Chermak, 1995). As a result, they maintain privileged status as the key definers of the crime problem and its solution (Hall et al., 1978). News organizations are dependent upon the police for a constant supply of crime information that comprises a large portion of the news. For this reason, news agencies often assign reporters to a "police beat" so they may obtain on-site information about the most recent crime incident. In turn, police organizations are dependent upon the news media to publicize crimes, request public cooperation with police investigations, and generate public support for additional law enforcement resources. Frequent and direct access to news media, therefore, often works to the advantage of police agencies, which receive generally favorable coverage. Although media evaluations of the entire criminal justice system are rare, Graber's (1980) content analysis of the *Chicago Tribune* suggests not only that police are evaluated more favorably in the press than are the courts and correctional system, but that stories are more likely to portray police performance as stable or improving than declining. More recently, Chermak (1998) reported results from a content analysis of more than 2,500 crime stories from both print and visual media. He concluded that most crime stories reflect positively on police performance by portraying them sensationally as crime fighters and emphasizing the dangers of police work.

As has been emphasized, however, throughout this text, police organizations are not immune to scandal, and during such times reporters may turn to non-official news sources for quotable sound bites. For example, Lawrence (1996) examined news coverage of police use of force in the *Los Angeles Times* between 1987 and 1992 to study the impact that two prominent media stories had on reporter reliance upon police as official and indexed news sources. She found that victims, their families, attorneys, witnesses to alleged acts of police brutality, and community activist groups became key media sources during times of exceptional or scandalous police events, often providing challenges to official interpretations of police misconduct.

The police-media relationship, therefore, is one that may be amicable in nature but also one that may sour at any given moment. Charged with the mandate of keeping watch on government officials, reporters often feel uneasy about their dependence upon police agencies, for they do not want to serve as uncritical publicists for police practices. Thus, reporters may temporarily abandon their dependence upon police during times of scandal, allowing other interested groups an opportunity to be critical of police authority. Recognizing this, police have traditionally been suspicious of the news media and continue to maintain a level of mistrust in their daily interaction with reporters (Chibnall, 1981; Garner, 1984).

The police approach to the news media, as well as their level of input into the newsmaking process reached a turning point in the 1960s when, for the first time, images of civil disturbances in cities like Los Angeles, Detroit, Newark and Chicago were broadcast across the nation. Not only were police ill equipped to handle protest and rioting on such a widespread scale, they were ill prepared to cope with media coverage of these non-routine events and unscripted police performances. With crime then the number one issue of concern among the public, President Johnson assembled the President's Commission on Law Enforcement and Administration of Justice to investigate criminal justice practices and to provide recommendations for improvement in the manner that police communicate to the public via media.

In addressing the need for improved police-community relations, the commission's *Task Force Report: The Police* encouraged police departments to establish an open dialogue with the press and other media, particularly through public relations officers (1967:159):

> Citizens who distrust the police will not easily be converted by information programs they consider to come from a tainted source. However, even for these groups, long-term education based upon honest and free dialogue between the police and the public can have an effect.

Two years later, the National Commission on the Causes and Prevention of Violence (1969:107-113) criticized media coverage of the recent urban riots as being sensational, but the commission report added that the inability of law enforcement to communicate effectively with reporters, especially in times of crisis, was a factor contributing to the level of violence:

> The press obtained much factual information about the scale of the disorders — property damage, personal injury, and deaths — from local officials, who often were inexperienced in dealing with civil disorders and not always able to sort out fact from rumor.

The report went on to recommend that law enforcement open up channels of information to the news media:

> Regular news conferences must be held...if they are not, the press will follow the sensational reports and fan the rumors. Members of the press, as feasible, should be permitted to...share in [official] evaluations in order to provide the facts to the public quickly and authoritatively. Regular formal contacts with the press should be augmented by frequent background briefings for community leaders because rumors flourish at all levels.

In 1973, the National Advisory Commission on Criminal Justice Standards and Goals (1973:44) advocated that police agencies promote an aggressive policy of proactively presenting information to the public rather than merely responding to media inquiries. To achieve this, police agencies should, "provide regular liaison between the agency and the media through an officer or unit, depending upon the size of the agency and the nature and frequency of local news media demands."

By the 1980s, police departments were once again reforming their organizational strategies. During the 1970s, studies such as the landmark *Kansas City Preventive Patrol Experiment* (Kelling et al., 1974) highlighted the limitations of preventive patrol and reactive policing, while research on foot patrols (Police Foundation, 1981) emphasized the impact that a positive police presence can have on citizen beliefs. It naturally followed that departments would begin to adopt a more community-oriented approach to public safety, one based upon proactive problem solving established through police-citizen partnerships. To accomplish this, a new proactive approach to confronting news media would be required, and the answer proposed was the establishment of police-media-relations offices staffed by professionally trained police-media spokespersons who could reach out to community members for public support while enhancing the overall image of law enforcement through actively participating in the newsmaking process.

MEDIA-RELATIONS UNITS: THEIR GROWTH AND FUNCTION

A media-relations unit is an office within a police organization that is responsible for handling communication with the news media. These offices are staffed by either civilian public information officers (PIOs) having an educational background in journalism and public relations or by sworn officers who may or may not have training in media communication. These offices are established to foster formal relations with members of the news media so that law enforcement may better serve the community through education of police practices and efforts. Media-relations offices also serve the interests of police, who are in a better position to shape the content of police-related news and exercise impression management. Until recently, few police agencies within the United States have had formal media-relations offices or employees whose primary task was media communication and impression management (Lovell, 2001). The confluence of live television and domestic unrest quickly made police public relations a new priority. New media formats demanded immediate changes to the way police patrolled urban environments. Today, a host of law enforcement organizations, including the Commission on Accreditation for Law Enforcement Agencies (CALEA) and the International Association of Chiefs of Police (IACP), are encouraging police departments to establish media-relations units staffed by individuals trained in media relationships, with each unit having a well-developed media-relations policy as part of the department's standard operating procedure. The goal is to encourage officers to confront the news media as potential law enforcement allies.

While the growth of police-media-relations offices within the United States is a recent development, they have been in existence for some time in England. One of the first police-press offices was established in 1919 in Scotland Yard, where communications between the police and the press occurred twice daily. Journalists had been placing bribes to police for information, and it was reasoned that establishing formal ties with reporters would curtail this practice. Of course, police officials also hoped that by providing the press with information, they could reduce opportunities for alternative interpretations of criminal events (Crandon, 1993). Over the next five decades police-media relations at Scotland Yard fluctuated from cooperative and open to secretive and hostile.

Then in 1972, Sir Robert Mark was appointed Commissioner of the Metropolitan Police. Appointed at a time when the force was faced with scandal, Mark decided that his force should have a relationship with the press marked by an unprecedented level of openness. Under his new policy, the police were to openly provide information to the media unless restricted by judicial order, to protect individual privacy, or to ensure the security of the state. Police were to issue press cards for the purpose of identifying accredited journalists, and officers likely to deal with the media on a regular basis were to receive training in media relations (Schlesinger and Tumber, 1994).

Mark's policy of openness with the media led to the establishment of formal police-media-relations units, and his policies would serve as a model for police-media-relations offices on an international scale. In the early 1980s, a series of reports on the reorganization of the Metropolitan Toronto Police called for the establishment of a public affairs department whose responsibility would include the development of improved relationships with the media. The department was charged with the task of providing information "consistent with the legitimate needs of the media" as well as the distribution of press releases and the development of police-media liaisons (Hickling-Johnston, 1982).

Today, media-relations units have become central to both the police organizational structure and the daily function of routine police work, and researchers are beginning to learn more about the functions and responsibilities of police-media relations offices and their PIOs. In an early study of police-media-relations in the U.S., Guffey (1992) surveyed 34 police departments from a national sample and interviewed 17 police chiefs for the purpose of eliciting proposals to improve police-media relations and, by extension, coverage of police practices. Results from his survey indicated that all selected police departments had an appointed media spokesperson, although some worked only on a part-time or "as needed" basis. Among the suggested proposals for improved media relations were the designation of a PIO in all departments, the adoption of a media-education training program for all officers, the development of a thorough media-relations policy, and PIO training in conflict resolution techniques.

Surette and Richard (1995) surveyed PIOs in Florida on their functions within the police organization and their training in media. They found that half of the PIOs surveyed had prior experience working in the mass media, and all received in-service training upon appointment. Their primary responsibilities were to handle inquiries from the news media, to arrange media interviews with other agency personnel, to distribute press releases, and to conduct press conferences and serve as the department spokesperson. The authors found that much PIO time was spent handling non-media related tasks. Thus, while PIOs may be full-time employees, they dealt with media often on a part-time basis. The authors concluded that much of the work of the PIOs surveyed is reactive in nature and does not entail prepackaging or proactive news creation.

In comparison to the American experience, Mawby (1997) surveyed the 43 Home Office-supervised police forces in England and Wales as part of a research project investigating police public relations. He found that 78% of forces reported having a media strategy whose stated objective was the promotion of the reputation of the force through both public information and public relations. Sixty percent of the media-relations offices were staffed with between one and five employees, with 93% providing in-force media training.

Chermak and Weiss (1999) examined the efforts made by police departments in the U.S. to promote community policing in the news. Specifically, they surveyed PIOs from 239 law enforcement agencies and found that 80% had at least one full-time official responsible for media relations. Each PIO had at least 50 hours of training in media relations. To promote the police, PIOs relied upon press releases and direct contacts with reporters. Their study also surveyed media managers about their receptiveness to PIO-initiated stories of police innovations, and found that reporters were able to provide coverage of police programs about 76% of the time.

Finally, a recent nationwide study of police-media relations funded by the National Institute of Justice (Lovell, 2001) reveals the nature and scope of police-media interaction as well as the routine responsibilities of the police-media-relations office and, specifically, the role of the police PIO. Conducted in the fall and spring of 2000, the study methodology produced what is probably the most comprehensive insight into the dynamics of police-media reflexivity, utilizing survey and ethnographic research to elicit both quantitative and qualitative information about the workings of police-media-relations office and the role of the police PIO. Specifically, a 10 page self-report survey inquiring about department media policies, procedures, and staff was distributed nationally to all municipal police departments in cities with a population of 100,000 residents or greater and produced a 76% response rate (194/255). Information garnered from the national survey was used to identify four police departments to serve as ethnographic case studies, where approximately 100 hours of observations of PIOs and their staff were conducted across four departments. The information that follows represents results generated from this study, the largest study of police-media relations PIOs in the United States to date.

Media Policies and Strategies

Ideally, organizations are goal-oriented, as goals provide the framework around which decisions and activities are directed (Simon, 1976). In order to achieve organizational success, it is often necessary for organizations to adopt a strategic model that will strive to guide administrative behavior. Among the strategies that often prove necessary is one that addresses communication with and through the mass media. For police, media communication has become increasingly important as it represents a primary means by which constituents view local law enforcement. As police are increasingly featured in the headlines of the news media, the ideal organizational strategy targeting media communication is one that successfully guides communicative behavior during routine policing events and — perhaps more importantly — during times of scandal when unsatisfactory police behavior is brought to the forefront.

Media policies have therefore become part of police standard operating procedures (SOP), dictating the nature of media communication. Specifically, these policies stipulate the type of information available for release, the parameters of media access during crime scene investigations, and when necessary, the chain of command to be followed regarding the release of information or statements to members of the news media. Results from the national survey indicate that 92% (n=177) of sampled departments had a written media policy as part of their agency's SOP. Yet the incorporation of media policies into police SOPs is a relatively recent occurrence. In fact, few departments (4%) had formal guidelines dictating media communication prior to the (1973) publication of reports of the National Advisory Commission on Criminal Justice Standards and Goals. Drafted in the aftermath of the televised urban unrest of the late 1960s and early 1970s, these federal reports recommended that law enforcement agencies incorporate an aggressive media policy into their daily operations. Police departments across the nation quickly adapted to the demands of television by adopting the recommendations of the National Advisory Commission (NAC) and devising guidelines to make media communication routine. In less than 10 years following the publication of the NAC report, the number of police agencies incorporating media guidelines into their SOPs increased three-fold; by the close of 1990, over 40% of all departments had adopted formal guidelines to communicate with and through the media.

While only 25% of sampled police departments identified a specific event prompting the formation of their department's media policy, of those departments that did specify an event, the largest number (28%) listed compliance with national accreditation standards. Among the other factors identified as prompting the adoption of media policies, 26% of departments indicated a change in police personnel as the primary factor, while 22% indicated increased police-media interaction as the catalyst. Finally, such factors as changes in state law, "the 1968 riots," and other "newsworthy events" complete the list of identified factors leading to the establishment of department media policies.

Because an overwhelming majority (75%) of responding departments failed to identify a specific event that prompted the adoption of a standard media policy, one can only speculate about the causes that brought about a heightened sensitivity toward the news media among police officials. Recent high-profile events, however, may have sparked an increased sensitivity among administrators who otherwise felt immune to the threat of extensive media coverage. For example, the 1991 beating of motorist Rodney King — caught on videotape and televised to an international audience — as well as the subsequent trial and rioting that it produced, may have triggered the formation of media policies in at least some of the departments. Over half of all police-media policies (51%) had been adopted in the years following the Rodney King incident, though again, there was no specific mention of the impact of this incident in open-ended survey responses. Still, whatever the actual causes, the past quarter century has experienced a growth in the capability of media technology that has been accompanied by a realization among police that interfacing with media is both politically necessary and desirable for community support. Recognizing that their image is shaped by the news media and that any given police action may quickly become public and newsworthy, police have adopted policies to ensure that their performances are anticipated, rehearsed, and otherwise routine.

Of course, *strategic* communication through media requires a high degree of planning and awareness on the part of the communicator. It calls for one to move beyond the mechanics of language and toward an understanding of situations and contexts, audiences and their opinions, and media demands and formats. A communicator may have any number of message objectives falling along a continuum from the most basic of goals to the most complex: a need to *inform the public*, a desire to *influence attitudes*, perhaps even a hope of *affecting behavior*. Those speakers most adept at achieving their personal or professional goals are those with an ability to integrate multiple communication objectives into their messages while delivering them through numerous forms of media (Garnett, 1992).

While the adoption of media policies was in response to an increasing sensitivity on the part of police toward how things might appear on television, few department policies make even a passing reference to requirements of reflexive policing, such as the police image, public relations, or impression management. Rather, the language of the typical policy reveals only the basic, single objective approach regarding media communication — "inform the public." As an example of a typical police-media policy, note the restrictive language in the following police department media policies:

> Members of [the Department] will assist the media with information, as long as the information does not compromise the investigation of a police incident; or detract from the ability to successfully prosecute a case in court; or violate an individual's legal right to privacy; or jeopardize the safety of any officer or citizen.

> It is the policy of [this] department to cooperate fully and impartially with the public and authorize news media representatives in their efforts to gather factual, public information pertaining to activities of the police department, as long as these activities do not unduly interfere with department operations, infringe upon individual rights, or violate the law.

Police-media policies, therefore, merely establish guidelines regarding the release of information. They provide little — if any — guidance on how to communicate in a strategic manner that both provides information and also targets audience perceptions of the police. Such duties are the responsibility of the police PIO, who serves as both a police department spokesperson and, when well trained, as the department public relations specialist.

POLICE PUBLIC INFORMATION OFFICERS

In an effort to improve police-media relations nationwide by engaging in a more proactive form of reflexive policing, the PIO has emerged as a key figure in police administration. Today, 89% of municipal law enforcement agencies have an employee whose primary responsibility is to serve as a media PIO, with 69% receiving at least some form of media skills training, though the variance is extremely high (mean=11 hours per year; median=5 hours; mode=1 hour per year). Employed predominantly as sworn officers (75%) and serving directly under the chief, PIOs represent the central source of information about department actions, and they act as spokespersons for the entire police force. Their objective is to facilitate the flow of information from the department to the media, avoiding information gaps that may cause reporters to depend upon less credible sources. Therefore, larger departments or departments in higher crime jurisdictions require their PIOs to be on-call around the clock. Having a police representative readily available to provide official and consistent information prevents what one large city chief referred to as, "rumors, lies or innuendos."

As the primary source of information on department operations, the PIO is responsible for all routine communication with members of the media. The PIO distributes daily crime incident information to reporters, prepares departmental press releases about agency events, responds to the scene of a police-related event where local media may gather, and arranges or provides assistance at police news conferences. To accommodate media inquiries for information on crime incidents, the PIO fields calls from beat reporters inquiring about any news events or developments on prior occurrences that may have transpired during the last news cycle. Depending upon the size of the media market, PIOs may receive anywhere from 10 to 30 inquiries each day, and more should there be a "breaking" event.

On routine days, the news occurs in cycles, and it is the responsibility of the PIO to meet the deadlines of various news formats. The PIO spends the morning hours prioritizing calls from area reporters, first responding to inquiries from broadcast reporters who require information for the rapidly approaching mid-day television broadcast. The heaviest volume of calls occurs in the hour just before airtime. The late afternoon is similarly spent preparing reporters for the evening news broadcasts, again with an abundance of calls placed just prior to going live. During the mid-day hours, then, the PIO finds much quiet time, allowing for the preparation of more proactive image building through the development of police-human interest stories, news "pseudo-events," or preparations for formal media interviews with the Chief.

When a crime or local emergency does occur, the PIO does not always represent the initial information gatekeeper. Instead, the on-duty dispatcher who is responsible for all field communication uses her discretion as to which calls may generate media attention. Following this initial screening, the dispatcher notifies the on-duty PIO via phone or pager regarding the nature of the incident. Once provided with this basic and initial information, the PIO will decide whether the event is newsworthy enough to warrant official notification of media. Of course, news editors monitor the same police radio frequencies as the dispatcher during their search for stories on local events; therefore, news assignment editors often come across police-related events without notification from the PIO and will dispatch a news crew to a scene without prior police contact. Other times, members of the community will choose to directly notify the media of a crime or major accident, forgoing any communication with the police. When this occurs, police beat reporters become the news gatekeepers, and it is not uncommon for police to first learn about breaking events from reporters themselves. In this case, the PIO is not the initial news gatekeeper, and she must instead use her training in media skills to apply to the day's event an interpretive news frame that best promotes the needs of the responding officers, the police organization, and of the community as a whole.

CONSTRUCTING NEWS FRAMES

For PIOs to successfully exercise impression management through the news media, they must possess an acute awareness of journalistic news framing. Typically, when police officers or political leaders complain about their actions or words being reported "out of context," they are essentially expressing their frustration over having lost control of the news frame. The problem for them is a failure to recognize that news is not merely reported, it is also interpreted. Absent any attempt by the PIO to provide the context of crime information, the department risks losing control of both information and public opinion. The challenge, then, as one PIO explained it, "becomes trying to take that negative thing and figuring out a way to put a positive spin on it so that...it's not focused upon negatively."

Routine News Events

Stories about neighborhood crime are considered "routine" news events when news coverage focuses upon details of the victims and of-fenders rather than on the justice system personnel (Graber, 1980). While it may seem somewhat inappropriate to refer to the occurrence of violent or tragic events as routine, for members of law enforcement it is the anticipatory nature of criminal events that qualifies them as such. That is, routine events represent expected occurrences that elicit planned responses. Crimes, crashes and natural disasters all qualify as routine events within the law enforcement community because they initiate an array of rehearsed, staged and planned responses on the part of police officials.

The Urbandale Police Department was adept at constructing inter-pretive news frames on otherwise tragic news events that reflected posi-tively not only upon the department, but also the broader community. As an example, a hit-and-run accident story became one of community heroism after a team of Urbandale PIOs deliberated at the crash scene and decided upon a news angle. The event began when an afternoon call came in to the Urbandale public information office regarding a hit-and-run that left a young boy in critical condition. Before responding to the scene, the staff issued a press release containing all initial information, though in all likelihood the news media were aware of the details before the Urbandale PIOs, since the news choppers were first to arrive at the accident site. Upon arrival, the senior PIO quickly spoke with each re-sponding officer to ensure accurate, complete, and consistent informa-tion.

A driver was speeding toward an elementary school zone when he encountered afternoon traffic at the end of the school day. The driver became impatient with the gridlock and decided to circumvent the traf-fic by bypassing all cars on the right. This resulted in the car careening upon the school sidewalk where it struck a mother standing with her two children, pinning the five-year-old boy underneath the car. After speaking with officers at the scene, the Urbandale PIOs learned that several witnesses to the crash had lifted up the car so that the child could be pulled out from underneath. With two of the assisting wit-nesses still nearby, the PIOs huddled and quickly decided upon the news frame: "Local Heroes Save the Day!" While at the accident site, one of the PIOs explained to the author their decision-making process:

> There are several angles here. First, you simply have the hit and run with the possible resulting homicide. There is also a story about what can result while speeding in a school zone. This is a safety issue we can focus on. Third, there is a story about Good Samaritans lifting a car to save a boy. Clearly, this third angle has the drama the media want. But ultimately, we can get three positive stories out of this one event. Today, we'll focus on the heroism and how lucky the boy is that members of the community come together. Especially in this high-crime community, they need a story like this. But tomorrow, we can focus on the fact that speeding in school zones will become a policing priority. Finally, if the boy does survive, and even if he doesn't, we will most certainly make the witnesses the local heroes of the month and gain additional positive media coverage when we give them their awards. I could push something else, but I decided on this one because I know the media, and media loves heroes. And picking a story angle like this one allows much media coverage of the heroes and encourages others to act accordingly.

When the stations went live and questioned the PIOs about the seriousness of the boy's condition, the Urbandale PIO responded by saying, "He's on his way to emergency now, but you know, I think the real story here is about our local heroes," and as he spoke, he directed the cameras to the "heroes" standing by his side, two local youths who were more than willing to take credit for their actions. The following morning, the newspaper metro section headline featured the angle proffered by the PIOs — "HEROES LIFT CAR TO FREE BOY" — while the subtext made passing reference to the tragedy of the event: "Young pedestrians hit, injured."

Accidents and Scandals

The role of the police PIO in promoting the image of the department becomes all the more important during times of accidents or scandals when the police are most vulnerable and face more intensive news coverage. Unlike routine events, which are events both planned and anticipated by police officials, "accidents" are events that begin as planned activities but result in unenvisioned happenings. That is, they constitute miscalculations that lead to a breakdown in otherwise routine events (Molotch and Lester, 1974). Similarly, "scandals" involve purposive yet out-of-character actions performed by individual players that are neither authorized nor intended for public view when they occur. Both accidents and scandals threaten the legitimacy of law enforcement when they befall police departments because their very occurrences are in direct conflict with the appearance of order, control, lawfulness and integrity. And because they result in that which is clearly not expected, they are attractive commodities as featured news items, especially when they involve agents of authority.

While police PIOs can — perhaps innocuously — create or highlight various news frames during times of routine policing events, their objective during times of accident or scandal is to transform *pre-existing* news frames into something less damaging to the reputation of the department. Erving Goffman (1959, 1974) argues that it is possible for participants in an event to transform primary frames into new, interpretive frames, thereby altering the understanding of previously occurring actions. While his list of techniques is both long and complex, perhaps the best means available is to over-communicate some events while under-communicating others. According to Goffman, this should not involve either the telling of lies or the staging of false fronts because such misrepresentations — if and when discovered — will only threaten the believability of all future communications. Instead, the transformation of pre-existing news frames requires that PIOs provide variations in focus that yield reanalyses of taken-for-granted events.

Note the following example from the Urbandale Police Department of a "successful" transformation of a news event that is clearly one containing elements of police mishap and tragedy into one that highlights elements of a love story:

> We had a situation a few months back where a police officer went to a scene and failed to secure his car. He left the car running, left his keys in the car, and goes to take care of a fight situation. Well, he arrests someone, handcuffs him, puts him in the back seat of the squad car, again fails to secure the car, and leaves that person unattended. That person's girlfriend then gets into the driver's seat of the police car, drives away the police car, goes through an intersection and hits an oncoming car, killing the driver.

Well, you know, the story can be several things. The story could very well have been, "it's the police's fault, it was negligence on the police officer's part and that negligence caused this tragedy to happen." And of course the lawsuits will follow. What we did was, we presented the story totally different. We presented the story as a "stand by your man" story. That the girlfriend would go to any lengths to protect him. So basically what we took, we took that story and presented it in a way that still says, yeah, this happened and that happened and that happened. But the story, the angle, is the fact that she stood by her man, taking the focus off those other things or at least overshadowing the focus on those. We fed the story to [the news media] the way we wanted it presented. There's an old saying that "information given is information controlled." And basically we neatly packaged it and gift-wrapped it and we gave it to them that way...This is a love story, and it's a tragic love story. It makes for great television.

Not all departments take advantage of the opportunities for public relations and spin control that a full-time media spokesperson can afford. The Union Creek Police Department serves a major city of comparable size to Urbandale but employs only one full-time PIO who does not receive any training in media communication or public relations, and it shows. Not only are the departments comparable in size, both departments experienced comparable incidents of officer malfeasance, but in only one case did the event become a media scandal. Both the Urbandale Police Department and the Union Creek Police Department had on their hands officers who were (allegedly) involved in the drug trade. Both departments investigated their own officers and even cooperated with federal law enforcement in their investigations. But where the Urbandale PIO decided to go public with the story and use it to the department's advantage by issuing a press release — and thereby framing the arrest as an attempt to clean house ("[Urbandale] Police Department arrested one of its own") — the Union Creek PIO did not go public with the arrest, and as a result could not control the news frame when the story was leaked to the press ("A [Union Creek] police officer stole $12,000 in a sting the FBI set up").

Another big city police department — the Morganville Police Department — has a public information office but fails to use it to proactively communicate with local reporters or to create public trust in law enforcement. Instead, they communicate to the media as little as possible, especially during periods of accident or scandal, as reflected in the statement of a local broadcast news cameraman:

> From my experience, it's been...extremely difficult when a police officer has done wrong and we try to pursue the story. It's really tough, and they make things extremely hard for us...[B]ut these people deserve to be on film just as much as any other person. Some of the stuff that some of the guys [on the force] have done are pretty serious...It's our job to show the public who the person is, and it's important because these are the people that are representing and supposed to protect us.

As a case in point, when an innocent man was mistakenly shot and killed in his own home by Morganville police, the PIO staff — as dictated by the chief — decided not to release any information about the incident. Thus, a press release issued by the Morganville police on the day of the shooting reads, "the homicide unit is currently conducting the investigation," with few additional details provided. Some two days after the shooting, the Morganville Police still had failed to disclose any information related to the shooting. A month after the shooting, the story failing to disappear, a local television station received a tip from some officers about what might have been the cause of the shooting. The papers were quick to pick up the story:

FATAL RAID ON WRONG HOUSE?
...AFFIDAVIT FALSIFIED

> Did [Morganville] police target the wrong house in a "no-knock" drug raid in which they shot a man to death? And if so, did they raid that house because of falsified information on a police affidavit? Those are among the questions being asked in the police and district attorney's investigation into last month's raid. [The suspect] was shot eight times by police officers when he reportedly refused to drop a pistol he was pointing at SWAT officers who had just broken in the front door of his home. Now, some officers, according to a Monday television report, are questioning whether some information in an affidavit supporting the search warrant was fabricated, questioning whether they entered the wrong house and killed [the suspect].

Commenting on the story, a Morganville PIO acknowledged the department's tradition of secrecy and attributed it to city politics, where department officials are discouraged from commenting on ongoing internal investigations. Nevertheless, s/he recognized the harm caused to the department's media image by a policy of silence, for a policy of silence prevents the construction of alternate news frames. According to the Morganville PIO, "Once someone has leaked to the media that the [Morganville] Police is investigating some particular internal matter," the task quickly becomes trying to respond and react to the appearance of "a cover up" in addition to the previously made allegations of misconduct. "And that's how we damage ourselves."

MEDIA-RELATIONS UNITS AND PIOS: AN END TO REFLEXIVITY?

The balance between the role of "public information officer" versus the public information officer as "press relations expert" poses a real challenge to law enforcement and a potential threat to police accountability. In a climate where the presence of media affords opportunities for the promotion of the police organization, PIOs must — above all — serve the public interest, and they must do this even when the information provided to the media reflects negatively upon the interests of the department. One PIO called attention to this paradox directly by acknowledging the concern that public information has the potential to inappropriately give way to public relations: "It's very important not to get the two jobs mixed up. Public information entails supplying reporters with accurate and truthful information. Public relations implies putting a 'spin' on information or the news." Of course, as police comfort with media communication improves, and as police are more willing to face their critics, the opportunity for reporter complacency arises. Skolnick and McCoy (1984:547) succinctly voice the growing concern that accompanies the development of sophisticated police impression management:

> Does the PIO's usefulness undermine the reporters' capacity to engage in objective and skeptical inquiry? Or at least, does the PIO's ready storehouse of facts about particular crimes subtly divert inquiry away from the processes and procedures of policing?

...The more qualified the police media specialist, the less independence the reporter may exert. As reporters become more dependent on the police department, they may lose the capacity to dig independently.

In other words, there is a very real concern that as police become more adept at *proactive* (i.e., promotional) media appearances, they may simultaneously be less likely to engage in meaningful and *reactive* (i.e., corrective) reflexive policing, for their media appearances will be designed to deflect pressure away from what the public deems as necessary organizational change. There are signs, though, that a willingness on the part of police to conform to the demands of media may yield some significant social benefits at the very same time that popular portrayals of law and justice may exert a negative influence upon the future of policing in a mass-mediated climate. The final chapter presents both consequences and contradictions of policing in an era of mass media.

NOTES

1. This chapter presents results from a national study on police public information officers conducted in the spring and fall of 2000, funded by the U.S. National Institute of Justice (2000-IJ-CX-0046). The names of both departments and personnel contained in this chapter represent pseudonyms.

2. Jackall, R. (1995). *Propaganda*. New York: New York University Press.

8. CONTRADICTIONS AND CONCLUSIONS: REFLEXIVE POLICING

It is 10 p.m. on a Tuesday evening, and citizens are cheering as the New York City Police do "whatever it takes" to make the streets safe again. Urban life is tough, and we have come to appreciate the police officer not intimidated by the legal barriers that plague contemporary police work. Perhaps this is why no one cried foul when Detective C. McDowell from the 15th precinct served as lookout while her partner beat information out of a strip club owner. Or why civil rights activists failed to take to the streets when homicide investigator D. Sorensen only received a temporary desk assignment for strip-searching and committing an aggravated assault on a young suspect. And when Detective A. Sipowicz secured a confession through deception and intimidation, who among us was going to complain? After all, we would not want it any other way.

It is 11 p.m. on a Tuesday evening. The TV show *NYPD Blue* has just ended and the local news broadcast has just begun. Citizens are now jeering at headlines of the real NYPD doing "whatever it takes" to make the streets safe again. Urban life is tough enough without having to watch out for the police officer who tramples constitutional protections and hard-fought-for civil rights. Perhaps this is why citizens cried foul upon the discovery of the 1998 beating of Haitian immigrant Abner Louima, who was stripped and then subjected to the most brutal of aggravated assaults. Or why civil rights activists took to the streets in protest of the shooting death of Amadou Diallo — an unarmed man who was shot 41 times. And when the NYPD's undercover deception led to the shooting death of Patrick Dorismond, many citizens complained. People want to be policed, but not this way.

MASS MEDIA AND THE PARADOXES OF POLICE WORK

Each day, politicians promise that through an expanded and better-equipped police force, law enforcement can *and will* make the streets safe for citizens. Amazingly, police have been placed at the forefront of social regulation after all other mechanisms of informal social control (i.e., family, peers, schools, social services, and churches) have failed. When this happens, police are called upon by community leaders to restore and maintain the social order while operating under the letter of the law. They are expected to make "split-second" decisions — so long as those decisions yield appropriate outcomes. And they are to avoid becoming hardened, cynical, or overly suspicious of the public they police, despite being trained in the use of firearms, tear gas, batons, and other crowd control techniques.

One of the paradoxes of contemporary police work (Perez, 1997), though, is that despite media imagery to the contrary, law enforcement and crime fighting occupy a relatively small part of what police actually "do." Yet popularly held expectations about what the police *should* be doing — expectations shaped in part by the mass media — place unrealistic demands upon police work. Perez (1997:2-3) captures the dilemma of the publicly held crime fighter myth rather succinctly in a series of rhetorically asked questions:

- Are the police law enforcers?

- If enforcing the law encompasses such a small part of police work, why should the profession even be labeled law enforcement?

- Don't the majority of all police calls involve solving family problems, breaking up bar fights, answering loud party calls, dealing with barking dog complaints?

Simply put, an emphasis upon crime fighting on the part of the police seems, as Perez puts it, "dangerously shortsighted." Yet it is an emphasis on the crime-fighting aspects of police work that both politicians and — in particular — news and entertainment media focus almost exclusively upon.

This paradox of the "police-as-crime-fighter" myth becomes all the more challenging when police must perform in the shadow of the mass media's fictional "good cop." Recall that the good cop is mere fantasy, defined not by professionalism but by effectiveness in crime-fighting ability. The good cop is the loner, the maverick, and the rogue officer unrestrained by bureaucratic red tape. S/he (but more typically "he") is always successful because the good cop need not be concerned with the legal handcuffs that restrain real law enforcement officers. The good cop also operates within a social order where morality is clearly dichotomized, with the officer always on the "right" side. Finally, the good cop is exceptionally popular, as evident in *NYPD Blue*, where fictional Detective Andy Sipowicz — a violent, racist and all around "dirty" cop — is celebrated by the viewing public as the show's key law enforcement hero. He coerces confessions, engages in backroom deals, and roughs up defendants, but always emerges successful in bring about a complete resolution.

A second paradox of police work in an era of mass media, then, is the popularity of the "fictional" rogue cop at a time when — in reality — the public are demanding a more accountable police force. The emergence of the rogue cop within entertainment media represents a relatively recent occurrence, with the most popular figure being that of Clint Eastwood's portrayal of "Dirty Harry." A persona that originated in the late 1960s but endured through the Reagan years of the 1980s, film historians (e.g., Clemens, 1997) locate the source of Harry's popularity in his violation of various U.S. Supreme Court decisions that limited police discretion. Thus, Harry is seen as part of a conservative backlash against the cultural liberalism that dominated much of the 1960s. But the rogue cop persona persists today, leading King (1999) to argue that the popularity of the aggressive cop taps into a broader sense of "losing ground" experienced by many in modern times, particularly white males. It is little coincidence, then, that these fictionalized loose cannons are more often than not middle-aged white guys struggling to survive in contemporary society. Still other explanations for the popularity of the rogue cop suggest that because he is constantly engaged in preposterous violence, his character serves as a form of escapism that no viewer could possibly take seriously (Twitchell, 1989).

To be sure, there is nothing genuinely fictitious about a television program like *NYPD Blue*. Perhaps the purest example of the contemporary cop drama, its only crime is that of exaggeration. The backdrop is real, as are the depictions of racial tension, urban angst, legal, ethical and bureaucratic "restraints," not to mention the program's incorporation of real New York headlines (e.g., the terrorist attacks of September 11, 2001 and the subsequent anthrax scare) into plot narratives. Even the photography uses documentary-like techniques, such as the incomplete headshot and the shaky/runaway camera, making an episode more likely to resemble the "reality-based" program *COPS* than the fabricated, campy melodrama of *CHIPS* from years past. It is, then, a program that is indicative of the condition of the hyperreal, a condition that also blurs the distinction between entertainment media's portrayal of the good cop and the idea of the good cop held by citizens when watching their evening news.

Whatever the explanation for the popularity of the fictional "good cop," it is important to take a moment to reflect upon the impact that the popularity of the loose cannon might have upon actual police practices. Like their predecessors who monitored the image of the Keystone Kops or G-Men in entertainment media, contemporary police officers pay close attention to both "real" and fictional depictions of law enforcement, and as Perez (1997) notes, they recognize that these images are often at odds with most forms of police work. This fact, however, does not stop the police from paradoxically trying to live up to their media image. Anyone who has ever had an opportunity to join the police in a ride-along has likely heard the police officer say something like, "I hope you get to witness some drama on the street tonight." In fact, after spending two years participating in police ride-alongs, Perlmutter (2000) concluded that police have a love/hate relationship of sorts with their fictional counterparts. They resent having to live up to the fictional image that they themselves have internalized.

While much of this book has focused upon the positive aspects of mass media and police reflexivity, problems with reflexivity may arise if cops do indeed feel as though the public expects them, at least on some level, to behave and perform like their television and cinematic counterparts and internalize these behavioral cues. This becomes especially problematic as the distinction between fictional and news media becomes increasingly difficult to detect, and when police on reality crime shows such as *COPS* patrol a world far more violent and dramatic than everyday crime reports would seem to suggest (Kooistra et al., 1998). Escapism or not, the popularity of the fictional "good cop" may come at a high price for the public if the consumption of escapist entertainment nevertheless promotes or appears to reflect false cultural expectations for everyday police performance.

CONCLUSION: FUTURE PROSPECTS FOR REFORM

"In an effort to make highway police more accountable," began a December 7, 1998 Associated Press wire story, "video cameras have been installed in more than 200 patrol cars on the New Jersey Turnpike."[1] The announcement was momentous, for it brought an end to a decade of denial whereby officials dismissed allegations that the state police engaged in racial profiling. In 1997, minorities accounted for 73% of people searched by state police on the turnpike; in the period covering 1994 to 1996, minorities represented 84% of all searches. Now, faced with a federal investigation into the state's practices, even the state's harshest critics expressed hope in the promise that a video camera mounted in each patrol car can put an end to racial profiling. New Jersey Governor Christie Whitman declared the in-car video cameras "an important tool that will help State Police preserve evidence of an accident or a crime scene." More importantly, though, "the cameras will also provide straightforward evidence of the law enforcement process, ultimately protecting both troopers and the public." Constitutional law professor David Cole agreed, noting that the incorporation of media technology into the patrol framework benefits everyone. "Accountability is key, accountability to both the public by the release of data and accountability within the department by making it possible for supervisors to track what an officer is doing."[2]

Recently, a big city police chief addressing an international gathering of law enforcement media spokespersons declared, "The future sees law enforcement becoming more and more transparent." The proclamation was momentous, for it capped a four-day conference dedicated exclusively to the principle that a thorough understanding of media must quickly become a policing priority. Speaking to a crowd of officials both foreign and domestic, and representing law enforcement agencies at all levels of government, the chief was emphatic that officers conform to the demands placed upon them by the technologies and formats of the mass media, declaring that police can "use drama to inform the public and still be accurate" (Lovell, 2001). By the same token, the words came a bit late and only echoed what some police media spokespersons had been saying for some time. As one police spokesperson put it (Lovell, 2001):

> [I]f...cops [don't like] this, then they had better go back to a time when TV didn't exist. Like it or not, we live in a media/video/showbiz world. We can either understand that and work with it or live in a bubble.

*   *   *

The message is becoming clear: the mass media are an inescapable component of everyday police work. Whether it is by incorporating media technology into their routine patrolling for the mass dissemination of images at a later date, or whether by employing public relations (i.e., "drama") into the delivery of public information, there is an increasing awareness on the part of law enforcement that those departments that conform to the demands of the mass media will maintain a more favorable public image, while those that fail to meet the demands of media will suffer politically. And it is a logical conclusion. Since the development and proliferation of the mass media, police have always been featured prominently in print, movies, comic books, television, and the news. The drama of policing, the mythology of the crime-fighter persona, and the enormous authority that comes with the job render the police popular features in both news and entertainment. Police can either co-opt their media mystique by putting it to their advantage through proactive, reflexive monitoring of media imagery, or they can do nothing until the inevitable scandal befalls their agency.

The dramaturgical aspect of policing, though, is really nothing new. As Manning (1997) illustrates, police work has always been predicated upon the promotion and performance of an image. The literature on policing too is filled with examples of dramaturgical allusions. Law enforcement textbooks talk about police "performance," "staged" operations and the "drama" on the street. The "blue curtain" and the "thin blue line" serve as a referent to the imagined wall that separates police from the public and performer from audience. Even the very nature of police work is described less as a job than a "role," where the "permanent rehearsal" that constitutes policing requires that officers "cast" themselves as obedient soldiers.

At the same time, if police have always been performers of sorts, likewise the mass media have traditionally performed an important policing function. In fact, the policing of public officials by the mass media is inextricably linked to the media's very inception. According to Emery's (1962) interpretive history of journalism, with the birth of the printing press came a new dimension to democracy as the press made a record of official actions for all citizens to see. He notes that in the British colonies mass-produced dailies were essential to the formation of a revolutionist movement, and upon the ratification of the U.S. Constitution a free press having the ability to monitor government actions was essential to the establishment and maintenance of a just society. Today, newspapers and independent reporters are still uncovering and reporting cases of police misconduct, such as the corruption that plagued the LAPD's Rampart Division. Moreover, the freedoms of the press to police government officials also extends to entertainment media as well, as exemplified by both the book and movie versions of *Serpico* and *All the President's Men* (works depicting true accounts of misconduct in law enforcement and the federal government, respectively).

With the invention and proliferation of new forms of media technology since the early days of the press, never before has information about the police been accessible to so many people on so many occasions, rendering the police increasingly vulnerable to public scrutiny in the face of perceived misconduct. As a result, police are indeed accentuating the positive aspects of routine police work. They are making themselves available to reporters through the establishment of media-relations units and the hiring and training of police PIOs. They are engaging in proactive and reflexive policing through their co-optation of video cameras now mounted within squad cars. And as a result of this high level of media exposure, they are making themselves more accountable to the very public they serve. Yet while police are increasingly appearing in the media spotlight, they are also becoming more adept at engaging in spin control and playing for the camera. As discussed in the previous chapter, police today are beginning to receive the same media and public relations training skills taught to the private sector. All of this poses very real problems for the existence of a more open police department that is simultaneously more publicly accountable.

As society moves forward into the information age, policing increasingly occurs in a climate dominated by the mass mediated "hyperreal."

In this climate, the line between the real and the fictitious becomes all the more permeable. Real cops are the stars of their own entertainment television program (e.g., *COPS*), and police officials are trained public relations specialists. In the mediated society of the new century, reality crime shows mask as police dramas, and police dramas serve as a proxy for reality. All of this makes the prospects for meaningful police reflexivity problematic. Watching television or reading the daily paper, it is becoming increasingly difficult to determine whether reality is a reflection of the fictitious, or whether the fictitious is a reflection of the real. And this makes a rendering of what truly constitutes the good cop from the bad cop more difficult.

NOTES

1. "State Police Install Video Cameras in Turnpike Patrol Cars," by S. Mitra Kalita. Associated Press state and local wire, December 7, 1998.

2. "State Tells Court Racial Profiling Reforms Working," by John P. McAlpin. Associated Press state and local wire, November 1, 2001.

REFERENCES

Anderson, W.T. (1990). *Reality Isn't What it Used to Be.* San Francisco, CA: Harper & Row.

Asch, S.E. (1958). "Effects of Group Pressure upon the Modification and Distortion of Judgments." In: E.E. Maccoby, T.M. Newcomb and E.L. Hartley (eds.), *Readings in Social Psychology.* New York: Henry Holt.

Associated Press (2002). "Inglewood Begins Preparation for Verdict in Police Abuse Case." October 14. (Retrieved from: http://www.sfgate.com.)

Bagdikian, B. (2000). *The Media Monopoly.* Boston, MA: Beacon Press.

Balch, R.W. (1972). "The Police Personality: Fact or Fiction?" *Journal of Criminal Law, Criminology and Police Science* 63(1):106-119.

Banfield, E.C. (1970). *The Unheavenly City: The Nature and Future of Our Urban Crisis.* Boston, MA: Little Brown.

Barak, G. (1988). "Newsmaking Criminology: Reflections on the Media, Intellectuals, and Crime." *Justice Quarterly* (5)4:565-567.

Barille, L. (1984). "Television and Attitudes About Crime: Do Heavy Viewers Distort Criminality and Support Retributive Justice?" In: R. Surette (ed.), *Justice and the Media.* Springfield, IL: Charles C Thomas.

Baudrillard, J. (1996). *The Perfect Crime.* New York: Verso.

—— (1983). *Simulations.* New York: Semiotext.

Baxter, J. (1970). *The Gangster Film.* New York: A.S. Barnes.

Bayley, D.H. and H. Mendelsohn (1971). *Minorities and the Police: Confrontation in America.* New York: The Free Press.

Bell, D. (1961). *The End of Ideology.* New York: Free Press.

Bennett, W.L. (1990). "Toward a Theory of Press-State Relations in the United States." *Journal of Communication* 40(2):103-125.

Berger, P. and T. Luckmann (1967). *The Social Construction of Reality.* New York: Anchor Books.

Bernays, E.L. (1923). *Crystallizing Public Opinion.* New York: Liveright.

Best, S. and D. Kellner (1991). *Postmodern Theory: Critical Interrogations.* New York: Guildford Press.

Bettmann, O.L. (1974). *The Good Old Days — They Were Terrible!* New York: Random House.

Blumer, H. (1986). *Symbolic Interactionism.* Berkeley, CA: University of California.

Boorstin, D.J. (1992). *The Image: A Guide to Pseudo-events In America.* New York: Vintage.

Buxton, D. (1990). *From The Avengers to Miami Vice: Form and Ideology in Television Series.* New York: Manchester University Press.

Carte, G.E. and E.H. Carte (1975). *Police Reform in the United States: The Era of August Vollmer 1905-1932.* Berkeley, CA: University of California.

Charney, L. and V.R. Schwartz (1995). *Cinema and the Invention of Modern Life.* Berkeley, CA: University of California.

Chermak, S.M. (1998). "Police, Courts, and Corrections in the Media." In: F.Y. Bailey and D.C. Hale (eds.), *Popular Culture, Crime and Justice.* Belmont, CA: Wadsworth.

—— (1995). *Victims In the News: Crime and the American News Media.* Boulder, CO: Westview.

—— and A. Weiss (1999). "Identifying Strategies to Market the Police in the News." Final Report Submitted to United States Department of Justice. National Institute of Justice. Grant #96 – IJ – CX00078.

Chibnall, S. (1981). "The Production of Knowledge by Crime Reporters." In: S. Cohen and J. Young (eds.), *The Manufacture of News: Deviance, Social Problems and the Mass Media.* Beverly Hills, CA: Sage.

Chiricos, T., S. Eschholz and M. Gertz (1998). "Crime, News and Fear of Crime: Toward an Identification of Audience Effects." In: G.W. Potter and V.E. Kappeler (eds.), *Constructing Crime: Perspectives on Making News and Social Problems.* Prospect, IL: Waveland Press.

Clarens, C. (1997). *Crime Movies: An Illustrated History of the Gangster Genre From D.W. Griffith to Pulp Fiction.* New York: Da Capo.

Cooper, L., E. Currie, J. Frappier, T. Platt, B. Ryan, R. Schauffler, J. Scruggs and L. Trujillo (1975). *The Iron Fist and the Velvet Glove: An Analysis of the U.S. Police.* Berkeley, CA: Center for Research on Criminal Justice.

Crandon, G.L. (1993). "Crime News: A Police Press Office — Police Press Perceptions." *The Police Journal* 66:242-255.

Crosby, J. (1949). "The Real McCoy." *New York Herald Tribune,* June 13. (Retrieved from: http://www.badge714.com/dragnyht.htm.)

Croteau, D. and W. Hoynes (2000). *Media Society: Industries, Images and Audiences.* Thousand Oaks, CA: Pine Forge Press.

Darnton, R. (1996). *The Forbidden Best-Sellers of Pre-Revolutionary France.* New York: W.W. Norton.

Davidson, E. (2000). *Reflections on a Disruptive Decade: Essays on the Sixties.* Columbia, MO: University of Missouri Press.

Davidson, W.P., J. Boylan and F.T.C. Yu (1976). *Mass Media: Systems and Effects.* New York, NY: Holt, Rinehart, and Winston.

Deakin, T.J. (1988). *Police Professionalism: The Renaissance of American Law Enforcement.* Springfield, IL: Charles C Thomas Publisher.

DeFleur, M.L. and S. Ball-Rokeach (1989). *Theories of Mass Communication* (5th ed.). New York: Longman.

Dominick, J. (1978). "Crime and Law Enforcement in the Mass Media." In: C. Winick (ed.), *Deviance and Mass Media.* Thousand Oaks, CA: Sage Publications.

Donnerstein, E., D. Linz and S. Penrod (1987). *The Question of Pornography.* New York, NY: Free Press.

Donovan, R.J. and R. Scherer (1992). *Unsilent Revolution: Television News and American Public Life, 1948-1991.* New York, NY: Cambridge University Press.

Douthit, N. (1975). "Police Professionalism and the War Against Crime in the United States, 1920s-1930s." In: G.L. Mosse (ed.), *Police Forces in History.* Beverly Hills, CA: Sage Publications.

Dove, G.N. (1982). *The Police Procedural.* Bowling Green, OH: Bowling Green University Popular Press.

Durkheim, E. (1951 [1979]). *Suicide: A Study in Sociology.* New York: The Free Press.

Edelman, M. (1975). *The Symbolic Use of Politics.* Urbana, IL: University of Chicago Press.

Eisenstein, E.L. (1997). *The Printing Revolution in Early Modern Europe.* New York, NY: Cambridge University Press.

Emery, E. (1962). *The Press and America.* Englewood Cliffs, NJ: Prentice-Hall.

Emsley, C. (1984). *Policing and Its Context 1750-1870.* New York: Schoken Books.

Epstein, E.J. (1974). *News from Nowhere.* New York: Vintage.

Ericson, R.V., P.M. Baranek and J.B.L. Chan (1989). *Negotiating Control: A Study of News Sources.* Toronto, CAN: University of Toronto.

Feagin, J.R. and H. Harlan (1973). *Ghetto Revolts: The Politics of Violence in American Cities.* New York: Macmillan.

Filler, L. (1976). *Appointment at Armageddon*. Westport, CT: Greenwood Press.

—— (1961). *Crusaders for American Liberalism*. Yellow Springs, OH: Antioch Press.

Fine, A. (1999). "In a Pursuit, Should Cops Let Bonnie and Clyde Go?" *The Christian Science Monitor*, August 24.

Fischer, C.S. (1992). *America Calling: A Social History of the Telephone to 1940*. Berkeley, CA: University of California.

Fisher, I. (1993). "Kelly Bans Choke Holds By Officers." *The New York Times*, November 24, Section B:1.

Fishman, M. (1980). *Manufacturing the News*. Austin, TX: University of Texas.

Fiske, J. (1995). *Understanding Popular Culture*. New York: Routledge.

Flynt, J. (1907 [1971]). "Corporation and Police Partnership with Criminal Pool-Rooms." *Cosmopolitan*, June 1907. In: H. Swados (ed.), *Years of Conscience: The Muckrakers*. New York: World Publishing.

Fogelson, R.M. (1977). *Big-city Police*. Cambridge, MA: Harvard University Press.

Fuchs, C. (2003). "Dragnet: PopMatters Television Review: Like a Virus." (Retrieved at: www.popmatters.com.)

Gamson, W.A. and A. Modigliani (1989). "Media Discourse and Public Opinion on Nuclear Power." *American Journal of Sociology* 95(1):1-37.

Gans, H.J. (1979). *Deciding What's News: A Study of CBS Evening News, NBC Nightly News, Newsweek and Time*. New York: Vintage Books.

Gardner, G. (1987). *The Censorship Papers: Movie Censorship Letters from the Hays Office 1934-1968*. New York: Dodd, Mead and Company.

Garner, G.W. (1984). *The Police Meet the Press*. Springfield, IL: Charles C Thomas.

Garnett, J.L. (1992). *Communicating for Results in Government: A Strategic Approach for Public Managers*. San Francisco, CA: Jossey-Bass.

Garza, M. (2003). "LAPD Changes Direction on Hot Pursuits." *The Daily News of Los Angeles*, Valley Edition, January 8, N1.

Geller, W., R. Nimocks, H. Goldstein and M. Rodriguez (1994). "Four Decades of Policing in Chicago." *Police Forum* 4:4.

Gerbner, G. and L. Gross (1976) "Living with Television: The Violence Profile." *Journal of Communication* 26:173-199.

Gest, T. (2001). *Crime & Politics: Big Government's Erratic Campaign for Law and Order*. New York: Oxford University Press.

Giddens, A. (1990). *The Consequences of Modernity*. Stanford, CA: University Press.

Giedion, S. (1955). *Mechanization Takes Command.* New York: Oxford University.

Goffman, E. (1974). *Frame Analysis.* Cambridge, MA: Harvard.

—— (1959). *The Presentation of Self in Everyday Life.* New York: Anchor Books.

Goldstein, H. (1977). *Policing a Free Society.* Cambridge, MA: Ballinger.

Gorn, E.J. (1995). "The Wicked World: The National Police Gazette and Gilded-Age America." In: C.L. LaMay and E.E. Dennis (eds.), *The Culture of Crime.* New Brunswick, NJ: Transaction.

Graber, D.A. (1997). *Mass Media and American Politics.* Washington, DC: Congressional Quarterly.

—— (1980). *Crime News and the Public.* New York: Praeger.

Graff, H.J. (1991). *The Legacies of Literacy: Continuities and Contradictions in Western Culture and Society.* Bloomington, IN: Indiana University Press.

Guffey, J.E. (1992). "The Police and the Media: Proposals for Managing Conflict Productively." *American Journal of Police* 11(1):33-51.

Hall, S., C. Critcher, T. Jefferson, J. Clarke and B. Roberts (1978). *Policing the Crisis: Mugging, the State, and Law and Order.* New York, NY: MacMillan.

Haller, M.H. (1976). "Historical Roots of Police Behavior, Chicago 1890-1925." *Law and Society Review* 10(2):303-323.

Hallin, D. (2001). "The Turning Point that Wasn't." In: R. Giles and R.W. Snyder (eds.), *1968: Year of Media Decision.* New Brunswick, NJ: Transaction. Publishers.

Harring, S.L. (1986). "Policing a Class Society: The Expansion of the Urban Police in the Late Nineteenth and Early Twentieth Centuries." In: D.F. Greenberg (ed.), *Crime and Capitalism: Readings in Marxist Criminology.* Philadelphia, PA: Temple University Press.

Harrison, J.M. and H.H. Stein (1973). *Muckraking: Past, Present and Future.* University Park, PA: Pennsylvania State University.

Havelock, E.A. (1963). *Preface to Plato.* Cambridge, MA: Harvard University Press.

Hickling-Johnston Limited (1982). *Metropolitan Toronto Police Management Study: A New Organization Design for the Metropolitan Toronto Police — Organizing to Meet the Challenges of the 1980's.* Toronto, CAN: Hickling-Johnston Limited.

Hilfer, T. (1990). *The Crime Novel.* Austin, TX: University of Texas.

Hodges, A. (2003). "Sgt. Friday Returns to His Beat." *Houston Chronicle,* January 30, p.2.

Innis, H.A. (1951). *The Bias of Communication.* Toronto, CAN: University of Toronto.

Jackall, R. (1995). *Propaganda.* New York: New York University Press.

Jarvie, I.C. (1978). *Movies as Social Criticism: Aspects of Their Social Psychology.* Metuchen, NJ: Scarecrow Press.

Jefferis, E.S., R.J. Kaminski and S. Holmes (1997). "The Effect of a Videotaped Arrest on Public Perceptions of Police Use of Force." *Journal of Criminal Justice* 25:5:381-395.

Jo, E. and L. Berkowitz (1994). "A Priming Effect Analysis of Media Influences: An Update." In: J. Bryant and D. Zillmann (eds.), *Media Effects: Advances in Theory and Research.* Hillsdale, NJ: Lawrence Erlbaum Associates.

Jones, C. (1993). *How To Speak TV, Print and Radio.* Tampa, FL: Video Consultants, Inc.

Kaminiski, R.J, R.S. Jefferis, S. Holmes and D.E. Hanley (1997). "The Effect of a Violent Televised Arrest on Public Perceptions of Police Use of Force." *Journal of Criminal Justice* 25(5):381-395.

Kappeler, V.E., M. Blumberg and G.W. Potter (1998). *The Mythology of Crime and Criminal Justice.* Prospect, IL: Waveland Press.

Katz, E. and P.F. Lazarsfeld (1955). *Personal Influence: The Part Played by People in the Flow of Mass Communication.* Glencoe, IL: Free Press.

Kelling, G.L. and K. Coles (1996). *Fixing Broken Windows.* New York, NY: Free Press.

—— and M.H. Moore (1988). "The Evolving Strategy of Policing." *Perspectives on Policing,* no. 4. Washington, DC: National Institute of Justice.

—— T. Pate, D. Dieckman and C.E. Brown (1974). *The Kansas City Preventive Patrol Experiment: A Technical Report.* Washington, DC: Police Foundation.

Kidd-Hewitt, D. and R. Osborne (1995). *Crime and the Media: The Post-modern Spectacle.* East Haven, CT.: Pluto Press.

King, N. (1999). *Heroes in Hard Times: Cop Action Movies in the U.S.* Philadelphia, PA: Temple University Press.

Knapp Commission (1973). *The Knapp Commission Report on Police Corruption.* New York: G. Braziller.

Kooistra, P.G., J.S. Mahoney and S.D. Westervelt (1998). "The World of Crime According to 'COPS'." In: M. Fishman and G. Cavender (eds.), *Entertaining Crime: Television Reality Programs.* Hawthorne, NY: Aldine de Gruyter.

Kramer, P. (2001). "'Clean, Dependable Slapstick': Comic Violence and the Emergence of Classical Hollywood Cinema." In: J.D. Slocum (ed.), *Violence and American Cinema*. New York: Routledge.

Lahue, K.C. and T. Brewer (1972). *Kops and Custards: The Legend of Keystone Films*. Norman, OK: University of Oklahoma Press.

Lane, R. (1967). *Policing the City: Boston 1822-1885*. Cambridge, MA: Harvard University.

Lang, G.E., and K. Lang (1972). "Some Pertinent Questions on Collective Violence and the News Media." *Journal of Social Issues* 28(1):93-110.

Lasley, J.R. (1994). "The Impact of the Rodney King Incident on Citizen Attitudes Toward Police." *Policing and Society* 3(4):245-255.

Lasswell, H.D. (1927). *Propaganda Technique in the World War*. New York: Alfred A. Knopf.

Lawrence, R.G. (1996). "Accidents, Icons, and Indexing: The Dynamics of News Coverage of Police Use of Force." *Political Communication* 13:437-454.

Lawrence, R. (2000). *The Politics of Force: Media and the Construction of Police Brutality*. Berkeley, CA: University of California.

Lazarsfeld, P., B. Berelson and H. Gaudet (1968). *The People's Choice: How the Voter Makes Up His Mind in a Presidential Campaign*. New York: Columbia University Press.

Lippmann, W. (1922 [1997]). *Public Opinion*. New York: Touchstone.

—— (1914 [1968]). "The Themes of Muckraking." In: H. Shapiro (ed.), *The Muckrakers and American Society*. New York: Mitchell Kennerley.

Loader, I. (1997). "Policing and the Social: Questions of Symbolic Power." *British Journal of Sociology* 48(1):1-18.

Loseke, D.R. (1999). *Thinking About Social Problems*. New York: Aldine de Gruyter.

Lovell, J.S. (2002). "Nostalgia, Comic Books, and the 'War Against Crime'! An Inquiry into the Resurgence of Popular Justice." *Journal of Popular Culture* 36(2):335-351.

—— (2001). "Police Performances: A Study of Police Organizations and Media Relations." Final Report (2000-IJ-CX-0046). Washington, DC: National Institute of Justice.

Lule, J. (2001). *Daily News, Eternal Stories: The Mythological Role of Journalism*. New York: Guildford.

Lyotard, J. (1997). *The Postmodern Condition: A Report on Knowledge.* Minneapolis: University of Minnesota.

Manning. P.K. (2001). "Police and Reflection." In: R. Dunham and G. Alpert (eds.), *Critical Issues in Policing: Contemporary Readings.* Prospect Heights, IL: Waveland Press.

—— (1997). *Police Work: The Social Organization of Policing.* Prospect Heights, IL: Waveland Press.

Marx, K. (1844 [1988]). *Economic and Philosophic Manuscripts of 1844,* translated by Martin Milligan. New York: Prometheus Books.

Mastrofski, S. (1983). "The Police and Noncrime Services." In: G.P. Whitaker and C.D. Phillips (eds.), *Evaluating the Performance of Criminal Justice Agencies.* Beverly Hills, CA: Sage Publications.

Mawby, R. (1997). *Survey of Police Media and Public Relations Offices.* Stafford, UK: Centre for Public Services Management and Research.

McChesney, R.W. (2000). *Rich Media, Poor Democracy: Communication Politics in Dubious Times.* New York, NY: The New Press.

McCombs, M. and D.L. Shaw (1972). "The Agenda-Setting Function of the Mass Media." *Public Opinion Quarterly* 36:176-187.

McLuhan, M. (1964). *Understanding Media: The Extensions of Man.* New York: New American Library.

Mestas, A. (2003). "TV Review: Dragnet." (Retrieved at: www.lightsoutfilms. com.)

Meyrowitz, J. (1986). *No Sense of Place: The Impact of Electronic Media on Social Behavior.* New York: Oxford.

Milgram, S. (1974). *Obedience to Authority.* New York: Harper and Row.

Miller, W.B. (1975). "Police Authority in London and New York City 1830-1870." *Journal of Social History* (Winter): 81-101.

Minow, N. and C.L. Lamay (1995). *Abandoned in the Wasteland: Children, Television, and the First Amendment.* New York: Hill and Wang.

Mills, C.W. (1968). *The Power Elite.* New York: Oxford.

Moyer, D. and E. Alvarez (2001). *Just the Facts, Ma'am': The Authorized Biography of Jack Webb.* Santa Ana, CA: Seven Locks Press.

Mulvey, L. (1973). "Visual Pleasure and Narrative Cinema." *Screen* 16(3):6-18.

Mumford, L. (1934). *Technics and Civilization.* New York, NY: Hartcourt Brace.

Munby, J. (1999). *Public Enemies, Public Heroes: Screening the Gangster from Little Caesar to Touch of Evil.* Chicago, IL: University of Chicago Press.

National Advisory Commission on Civil Disorders (1968). *Report.* (Kerner Commission.) Washington, DC: U.S. Government Printing Office.

National Advisory Commission on Criminal Justice Standards and Goals (1973). *The Police.* Washington, DC: U.S. Government Printing Office.

National Commission on the Causes and Prevention of Violence (1969). *Mass Media and Violence,* vol. XI. Washington, DC: U.S. Government Printing Office.

National Commission on Law Observance and Enforcement (1931 [1968]). *Report on Lawlessness in Law Enforcement.* (No. 11.) (Wickersham Commission.) Montclair, NJ: Patterson Smith.

—— (1931 [1968]). *Report on Police.* (No. 14.) (Wickersham Commission.) Montclair, NJ: Patterson Smith.

National Institute of Mental Health (1982). *Television and Behavior: Ten Years of Scientific Progress and Implications for the Eighties.* (Vol. 1: Summary Report.) Washington, DC: Government Printing Office.

NBC4 (October 22, 2002). "Hundreds Protest Against Police Shootings: March Part of National Day of Protest." (Available at: http://www.nbc4.tv/news/1733261/detail.html.)

Newsweek (1952). "Detective Story." January 14.

Niederhoffer, A. (1969). *Behind the Blue Shield: The Police in Urban Society.* New York, NY: Doubleday and Co.

Ortega, T. (2002). "To Protect and Swerve." *New Times Los Angeles,* May 9.

Oumano, E. (1985). *Film Forum: Thirty-Five Top Filmmakers Discuss Their Craft.* New York, NY: St. Martin's Press.

Owen, R. (2003). "ABC Hopes to Arrest Ratings Slump with Wolf's 'Dragnet'." *Post-Gazette,* January 13. (Retrieved from: www.post-gazette.com.)

Parks, B.C. (2000). *Rampart Area Corruption Incident.* (Executive Summary.) Los Angeles, CA: Los Angeles Police Department.

Parrington, V.L. (1926 [1968]). "A Chapter in American Liberalism." In: H. Shapiro (ed.), *The Muckrakers and American Society.* Lexington, MA: D.C. Heath and Company.

Perez, D.W. (1997). *The Paradoxes of Police Work: Walking the Thin Blue Line.* Incline Village, NV: Copperhouse Publishing.

Perlmutter, D.D. (2000). *Policing the Media: Street Cops and Public Perceptions of Law Enforcement.* Thousand Oaks, CA: Sage.

Petty, R.E. and J.R. Priester (1994). "Mass Media Attitude Change: Implications of the Elaboration Likelihood Model of Persuasion." In: J. Bryant and D. Zillmann (eds.), *Media Effects: Advances in Theory and Research*. Hillsdale, NJ: Lawrence Erlbaum Associates.

Police Foundation (1981). *The Newark Foot Patrol Experiment.*: Washington, DC.

Postman, N. (1994). *The Disappearance of Childhood*. New York: Vintage.

Potter, C.B. (1996). *War on Crime: Bandits, G-Men, and the Politics of Mass Culture*. New Brunswick, NJ: Rutgers.

Potter, J. (1996). *Representing Reality: Discourse, Rhetoric and Social Construction*. Thousand Oaks, CA: Sage Publications.

Poveda, T.G. (1982). "The FBI and Domestic Intelligence: Technocratic or Public Relations Triumph?" *Crime and Delinquency* 28(2):194-210.

Powers, R.G. (1983). *G-Men: Hoover's FBI In American Popular Culture*. Carbondale, IL: Southern Illinois University.

President's Commission on Law Enforcement and Administration of Justice (1967). *Task Force Report: The Police*. Washington, DC: U.S. Government Printing Office.

Price, B.R. (1977). *Police Professionalism*. Lexington, MA: D.C. Heath and Company.

Rafter, N. (2000). *Shots in the Mirror: Crime Films and Society*. New York: Oxford University Press.

Reiner, R. (1992). *The Politics of the Police*. Toronto, CAN: University of Toronto.

Reiss, A.J., Jr. (1971). *The Police and the Public*. New Haven, CT: Yale.

Reppetto, T.A. (1978). *The Blue Parade*. New York, NY: The Free Press.

Rosow, E. (1978). *Born to Lose: The Gangster Film in America*. New York: Oxford University Press.

Schlesinger, P. and H. Tumber (1994). *Reporting Crime: The Politics of Criminal Justice*. Oxford: Clarendon.

Schudson, M. (1996). *The Power of News*. Cambridge, MA: Harvard University Press.

Schwennesen, T. (2000). "Police OK New Tear Gas Policy." *The Register Guard*, March 1. (Retrieved at www.registerguard.com.)

Sears, D.O. and J.B. McConahay (1973). *The Politics of Violence: The New Urban Blacks and the Watts Riot*. Boston, MA: Houghton Mifflin Company.

Sennett, M. (1954). *King of Comedy*. Garden City, NY: Doubleday.

Serrano, R.A. and J. Rainey (1992). "Williams Sworn In as Chief, Calls for Healing LAPD." *The Los Angeles Times,* July 1.

Shapiro, H. (1968*). The Muckrakers and American Society.* Boston, MA: D.C. Heath.

Sherizen, S. (1978). "Social Creation of Crime News: All the News Fitted to Print." In: C. Winick (ed.), *Deviance and Mass Media.* Beverly Hills, CA: Sage.

Shuster, B. and A. Gorman (2002). "2 Policemen Indicted in Boy's Beating: 2 Officers Face Felony Counts," *Los Angeles Times,* Orange County Edition, July 18, A1, A27.

Simon, H.A. (1976). *Administrative Behavior: A Study of Decision-Making Processes in Administrative Organization.* New York, NY: Free Press.

Sklar, R. (1975). *Movie-Made America: A Cultural History of American Movies.* New York: Vintage.

Skolnick, J. (1975). *Justice Without Trial.* New York, NY: Wiley and Sons.

—— (1974). "The Police View of Protest and Protesters." In: A. Platt and L. Cooper (eds.), *Policing America.* Englewood Cliffs, NJ: Prentice-Hall.

—— and C. McCoy (1984). "Police Accountability and the Media." *American Bar Foundation Research Journal* 1984(3):521-557.

Slocum, J.D. (2001). *Violence and American Cinema.* New York: Routledge.

Smith, G. and J.B. Smith (1972). *The Police Gazette.* New York: Simon and Schuster.

Sorrentino, F.M. (1985). *Ideological Warfare: The FBI's Path Toward Power.* Port Washington, NY: Associated Faculty Press.

Sparrow, M.K., M.H. Moore and D.M. Kennedy (1990). *Beyond 911: A New Era for Policing.* New York: Basic Books.

Steinberg, S. (1961). *Five Hundred Years of Printing.* Baltimore, MD: Penguin Books.

Sullivan, W.C., with W. Brown (1979). *The Bureau: My Thirty Years In Hoover's FBI.* New York: W.W. Norton.

Surette, R. (1998). *Media, Crime, and Criminal Justice: Images and Realities.* Belmont, CA: Wadsworth.

—— (1995). "A Serendipitous Finding of a News Media History Effect." *Justice Quarterly* 12(2):355-364.

—— and A. Richard (1995). "Public Information Officers: A Descriptive Study of Crime News Gatekeepers." *Journal of Criminal Justice* 23:325-336.

Surgeon General's Scientific Advisory Committee on Television and Behavior (1972). *Television and Social Behavior.* (Reports and Papers, Volume III: Television and Adolescent Aggressiveness.) Washington, DC: U.S. Government Printing Office.

Swados, H. (1971). *Years of Conscience: The Muckrakers.* New York: World Publishing.

Theoharis, A.G. and J.S. Cox (1988). *The Boss: J. Edgar Hoover and the Great American Inquisition.* Philadelphia, PA: Temple.

Thompson, J. (1993). *Fiction, Crime, and Empire: Clues to Modernity and Postmodernism.* Urbana, IL: University of Illinois Press.

Treat, R. (1945). *V as in Victim.* New York: Duell, Sloan & Pearce, Inc.

Tuch, S.A. and R. Weitzer (1997). "Racial Differences in Attitudes Toward the Police." *Public Opinion Quarterly* 61:642-663.

Turner, G.T. (1909 [1964]). "The City of Chicago: A Study of the Great Immoralities." *McClure's Magazine,* November 1909. In: A. Weinberg and L. Weinberg (eds.), *The Muckrakers.* New York: Capricorn.

Turner, W.W. (1970). *Hoover's FBI: The Men and the Myth.* Los Angeles, CA: Sherbourne Press, Inc.

Twitchell, J.B. (1989). *Preposterous Violence: Fables of Aggression in Modern Culture.* New York: Oxford University Press.

Uchida, C.D. (2001). "The Development of the American Police: An Historical Overview." In: G.P. Dunham and R.G. Alpert (eds.), *Critical Issues in Policing: Contemporary Readings.* Prospect Heights, IL: Waveland Press.

Van Mannen, J. (1974). "Working the Street: A Developmental View of Police Behavior." In: H. Jacob (ed.), *The Potential for Reform of Criminal Justice.* Beverly Hills, CA: Sage.

Walker, S. (1980). *Popular Justice: A History of American Criminal Justice.* New York: Oxford University Press.

Walker, S. (1977). *A Critical History of Police Reform: The Emergence of Professionalism.* Lexington, MA: Lexington Books.

—— and C.M. Katz (2002). *The Police in America: An Introduction.* New York: McGraw Hill.

Warshow, R. (1962). *The Immediate Experience: Movies, Comics, Theatre, and Other Aspects of Popular Culture.* Garden City, NY: Doubleday.

Weber, M. (1958). *From Max Weber: Essays in Sociology,* edited by H.H. Gerth and C. Wright Mills. New York: Oxford University Press.

Weinberg, A. and L. Weinberg (1961). *The Muckrakers: The Era in Journalism that Moved America to Reform.* New York: Simon and Schuster.

Weisskopf, M. (1994). "Playing on the Public Pique: Consultant Taps Voter Anger To Help GOP." *The Washington Post,* October 27, 1994, A1.

Westley, W. (1970). *Violence and the Police: A Sociological Study of Law, Custom, and Morality.* Cambridge, MA: MIT Press.

Williams, R. (1977). *Television: Technology and Cultural Form.* New York: Schocken Books.

Wilson, H.S. (1970). *McClure's Magazine and the Muckrakers.* Princeton: Princeton University Press.

Wilson, J.Q. (1973). *Varieties of Police Behavior.* New York: Atheneum.

—— and G.L. Kelling (1982). "Broken Windows." *Atlantic Monthly,* March 1982.

Wilson, O.W. (1963). *Police Administration.* New York: McGraw-Hill.

Witcover, J. (2001). "Reassessing the Winners and Losers." In: R. Giles and R.W. Snyder (eds.), *1968: Year of Media Decision.* New Brunswick, NJ: Transaction Press.

Wolfe, T. (1972). "Foreword." In: G. Smith and J.B. Smith (eds.), *The Police Gazette.* New York: Simon and Schuster.

Wood, T. and F. Fiore (1991). "Beating Victim Says He Obeyed Police Law Enforcement." *The Los Angeles Times,* March 7.

Yaquinto, M. (1998). *Pump 'Em Full of Lead: A Look at Gangsters on Film.* New York: Twayne Publishers.

Zhao, J. (1996). *Why Police Organizations Change: A Study of Community-oriented Policing.* Washington, DC: Police Executive Research Forum.

Ziembo-Vogl, J. (1998). "Exploring the Functions of the Media in Community Policing." *Police Forum* 8(1):1-12.

Zinn, H. (1995). *A People's History of the United States.* New York: Harper Perennial.

INDEX

B

"Bad Cop," 15, 36, 41, 43-45, 102, 160
Baudrillard, J., 45, 46, 47

C

Chermak, S., 20, 134, 135, 140
Cinema, 9, 69-70, 79, 82, 83, 93-96
Civil Rights Movement, 107-110, 114, 126
Comic Books, 5, 31, 90, 91, 98, 112, 158
Crime Records Division, 90, 98
Cultural Lag, 10-12, 15, 65, 84, 98, 116

D

Dragnet, 31, 43, 102-104, 132

E

Entertainment Media, 5, 10, 20, 89, 90, 154, 155, 156, 159

F

Federal Bureau of Investigation, 3, 79, 81, 85, 86, 87, 89, 90, 92, 93, 94, 95, 96, 105, 117, 127, 149
Framing, 25, 29, 109, 145, 149

G

Gangster Films, 75-79, 93, 94
G-Men, 90, 91, 93, 95-96, 156
Goffman, E., 25, 148
"Good Cop," 15, 36, 41-43, 44, 45, 50, 79, 102, 155-156, 160
Graber, D., 20, 38, 67, 135, 146

H

Hays Office, 94, 95, 98
Hoover, J. Edgar, 79, 81, 84, 85-93, 94, 96, 98, 102, 118, 127
Hyperreality, 45-47, 91, 156, 159

I

Ideology, 24, 28, 29, 96
International Association of Chiefs of Police (IACP), 74, 80, 100, 129, 138

J

Jackson, Donovan, 2, 3, 29

K

Kerner Commission, 119, 124
Keystone Kops, 41, 71, 73-75, 80, 83, 156
King, Rodney, 1, 2, 3, 5, 7, 21, 29, 41, 142